Municipal Output and
Performance in
New York City

Municipal Output and Performance in New York City

David Greytak
Syracuse University

Donald Phares
University of Missouri-St. Louis

with

Elaine Morley
Syracuse University

Lexington Books
D.C. Heath and Company
Lexington, Massachusetts
Toronto   London

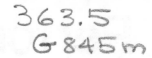

Library of Congress Cataloging in Publication Data

Phares, Donald.
  Municipal output and performance in New York City.

  Bibliography: p.
  1. Municipal services—New York (City)—Evaluation. 2. New York
(City)—Politics and government—1951-   . I. Greytak, David, joint author.
II. Morley, Elaine, joint author. III. Title
HD4606.N5P53   363.5   74-14415
ISBN 0-669-93682-0

Published simultaneously in Canada.

Printed in the United States of America.

International Standard Book Number: 0-669-93682-0

Library of Congress Catalog Card Number: 74-14415

To the Metropolitan Studies Program,
Syracuse University, and all those
who have been associated with it
and to Linda and C.L.L.

Contents

List of Tables

Preface

More and more, concern is voiced over what a citizen gets for his tax dollars, which become a part of the hundreds of billions of dollars expended on public programs. At every level of government, pressure is growing for greater accountability, efficiency, and performance. While steps have been taken to improve measurement of these concerns, much work remains.

Additional concern has arisen over issues that are directly linked to output in the public sector. Governmental reorganization hinges on issues like economies of scale, which require measurement of output. Equality in the provision of public services (such as education) mandates being able to define and quantify what one is relating "equality" to. The dollar, a widely used variable, is a very imprecise way of indicating what a governmental unit has accomplished. Government's purpose is not to spend money per se so much as to move toward goals and objectives that either cannot be entrusted to or cannot be accomplished by uncoordinated private activity. These issues all delineate the need for measurement of "those things that government does" and how well it is performing its responsibilities.

Of the three levels of government in our federal system, local government is the one most immediate to the citizen, most accountable for its financial operations, and least flexible in its fiscal structure. It is de facto caught in a needs-resources vise. On the one side is expanding pressure for spending to deal with all the problems that arise out of an advanced state of urbanization; on the other, it is constrained by taxpayer resistance to higher taxes, a shrinking resource base, severe political and fiscal limitations, and the squeeze of inflation and low productivity.

It is this milieu that sets the tone for this study. A modest attempt is made to document the provision of public services in New York City over the period 1960-73; it is by no means exhaustive nor exact, but it is suggestive of what went on. Output and performance are dealt with as those "things that government does" rather than as dollars spent or persons employed. As such, measurement is focused explicitly on the various facets or attributes of public services. New York City has been chosen for study since it manifests the most advanced (and in many ways the wealthiest) state of urbanization in the United States, with all that that implies. Also, it portends of a future condition for local government if certain forces are not recognized and dealt with appropriately. Perhaps it offers a view of things to come if we maintain the same drift course of events. Be that the case, we can profit from New York's current misery.

Acknowledgments

This study is an outgrowth of work begun while the authors were staff members of the Maxwell Research Project on the Public Finances of New York City at Syracuse University. Special thanks is due to Alan Campbell, dean of the Maxwell School, and Roy Bahl, director of the Metropolitan Studies Program, for their role in the overall research effort.

Acknowledgment is also due to Verdell Allen, Mary DeArchangel, Thessalonia Bunton, and Sandy Overton for their unfailing diligence in typing and preparing the manuscript, and to Brian Hayward for his last-minute research assistance. Last but by no means least special thanks is due to Norton Long for his continual support.

Part I:
Introduction

1

Measuring Output in the Public Sector

Overview

Measuring outputs from the public sector is an elusive endeavor, but one that consumes an increasing volume of academic, professional, and legislative attention. What the public sector does, at every level of government, has a pronounced impact on the quality of our lives and affects a wide array of private activities and future public policies. The question "How much and what is government producing?" is perfectly legitimate, but it may be overdue at the scale and intensity required.[a] No longer can we afford to take Adam Smith's stance that most government activity is unproductive, wasteful, and to be endured. Government has grown far too big.[b]

Perhaps of more immediate, individual concern are the activities undertaken, the taxes collected, and the funds spent by some 19,000 municipalities on the behalf of society at large and its citizens in particular. Local government is the political level most immediate to our needs, anxieties, and frustrations and is the one to which we turn when worry arises over the quality of education, the growth of crime, the adequacy of intraurban transportation facilities, the problems of pollution, and the like. More and more, it also acts as intermediary to handle relations with state and federal governments. Local government is, de facto, the element in our $400 billion public sector that has borne the brunt of urbanization-suburbanization in the United States and all the problems and issues that accompany it. Its very nearness makes its activities of even more concern since it remains the one level of government into which a citizen has some potential for direct input and occasionally even the power to say "yes" or "no," using, for example, the referendum.[c]

There is a clear need for quantitative and qualitative information on what local governments are doing with the billions they spend, $118 billion in 1972,[1] and, simultaneously, there are problems, both conceptual and empirical, that must be noted. Quantifying government output is a theoretical issue that has

---

[a]See, for example, Frank Levy et al., *Urban Outcomes* (Berkeley, California: University of California Press, 1974); *Social Science Quarterly*, vol. 54 (March 1974), special issue on "Measuring Urban Agency Output and Performance" and the various other studies cited therein.

[b]Refer to any text in public finance, for example, R.A. Musgrave and Peggy B. Musgrave, *Public Finance in Theory and Practice* (New York: McGraw-Hill, 1973).

[c]Note the public choice literature in Robert L. Bish, *The Public Economy of Metropolitan Areas* (Chicago: Markham, 1971).

plagued public finance specialists ever since attention shifted from the tax to the expenditure side of the budget.[d] Many of these issues remain in a state of flux. Joint consumption, lack of exclusion in consumption, no price or profit motive, coercion in payment, and separation of price (tax or cost) from goods received (expenditure or benefits) all greatly obfuscate the conceptual let alone the empirical issues.[2] Confusion at an empirical level is prevalent. Who receives the benefits, how many are received, and what they are are considerations even less settled than the question of who pays the taxes.[3] When we shift from dollars expended to actual measures of output we gain no additional conceptual precision but do benefit from additional detail on governmental operations.

Output from the public sector is not the final product sought by the taxpayer-consumer. Unlike the loaf of bread that we physically ingest, public output involves the "things" done through collective action to advance toward some desired end state, often vaguely specified, such as security, cleanliness, ease of access, heightened intellectual capacity, or better health. As citizens and taxpayers we are concerned with how these "outputs" become transformed into the "outcomes" that we desire.[e]

However, one set of outputs can lead to wide variation in the level of satisfaction it provides individual citizens. The fact that we obtain many public goods "in a lump" means that decisions in the public sector may be aimed at a median citizen—since we cannot satisfy all equally—with potentially wide variation around this median.[f] A citizen has the option of "voting with his feet" to find a basket of public goods closest to his tastes and preferences[g] or accepting, with frustration, what he gets, at least for the short run.

The need remains to obtain much more information on what the public sector provides in the way of output. Far too many crucial issues are being resolved without the benefit of the reality that such data might offer.

Issues Related to Output Measurement

The following is a listing of the kinds of matters that need measures of output for their proper specification and consideration:

---

[d]Look to any recent text in public finance for a discussion of this transition in academic attention, for example, as in note b.

[e]An *output* is something done or provided while an *outcome* is something we want accomplished, for example, police patrols versus crime prevention.

[f]Street lights, for example, are either present or absent. Once put in place their benefits are available to all. Education is provided *at some given level* (say as proxied by $1,000 per student); this may be far too much for some and far too little for others. An attempt is made to strike some balance around the tastes and preferences of a "median citizen."

[g]This has become known as the Tiebout model. Charles Tiebout, "A Pure Theory of Local Expenditures," *Journal of Political Economy*, vol. 64 (October 1956), pp. 416-24.

1. Outcomes-consequences
2. Efficiency
3. Effectiveness
4. Performance
5. Productivity
6. Goal attainment
7. Evaluation
8. Equity
9. Desirability
10. Public vs. private provision

This is not meant to be an exhaustive list nor are the categories mutually exclusive but they are reflective of major concerns related to public sector activity—concerns that mandate output measures to be considered appropriately.

Nature of the Public Sector

Government in the United States has become an integral part of our economic system. No longer do we exist in a capitalistic ideal and no longer does the "market" operate uninfluenced by what goes on in Washington, state capitals, or local city halls. A role for an active public sector has been clearly defined and movement in this direction is evident.

Richard Musgrave has segmented these responsibilities of collective action into three broad areas:[4] *Stabilization* attempts to cope with deviations in the performance of the economy, employment, growth, inflation, and balance of payments from some "desired norm." It accepts basic Keynesian notions that unemployment is inherent to any market-based economic system and may necessitate public intervention. *Distribution* relates to social concern over how the output from a market system is distributed to support its members. The crux of the issue is poverty and what to do about it; again public action may be deemed appropriate. *Allocation* focuses on the existence of positive and negative externalities that adversely influence private decisions to produce and consume. Collective action is undertaken here to cope with problems such as pollution, crime, traffic congestion, and zoning.

To follow Musgraves' nomenclature, we have delineated numerous issues that now fall under collective aegis in an attempt to deal with problems generated by but that cannot be adequately handled within a strict market setting, often referred to as *market failures*. We have in the process also instituted public support for a wide array of *merit goods*, which represent an intentional denial of consumer sovereignty in the interest of promoting the benefit of society at large. Cases in point are education, disease immunization, and police. Merit goods manifest collective concern to make available certain services that are absolutely essential and considered too critical to be delegated to the whims of individual choice and market forces. Once again the question arises as to the "outputs" that are derived from our tax support of public operations. We need empirical measures to be able to examine any of the output-related issues listed above.

Trends in the evolution of the public sector are shown in Table 1-1 and serve to underline the need for output measures beyond dollars spent or number of people employed; dollars and employees can be extremely deceptive indicators of what is actually being provided.[h] The average annual growth rate for the state-local sector between 1960 and 1973 exceeds that for the federal government along *every* dimension shown. Growth rate in purchase of goods and services is almost three times the federal rate of 20.6 percent, employment has risen nearly twice as fast, and the rate of increase in overall expenditures is about 50 percent higher at 20.9 percent. Relative to gross national product (GNP), differences between the two governmental levels are equally as pronounced. State-local expenditures as a percent of GNP have grown at an annual average rate of 3.4 percent, more than four times the federal rate. State-local employment growth has been positive and averaged 2.19 percent over the 13-year period while the federal rate has been a negative 1.3 percent. While the state-local sector may no longer be *the* "most dynamic sector," as suggested several years ago by Alan K. Campbell,[5] it remains one of considerable, sustained expansion both in expenditures and employment.

Responsibility in a Federal System

One of the issues that has and continues to plague those concerned with public sector activity and its increasing absolute and relative importance in our economy is the question of division of responsibility or assignment of functions—essentially it is a question of who can best do what in the context of a three-leveled, federal system? The factors entailed are complex and much attention has already been devoted to their comprehension. While their ultimate conceptual resolution is not at issue here, the problem has an intimate and direct bearing on any attempt at measurement of public outputs. As shown by the literature on the assignment question, measurement of output is of primal concern in any discussion of economies of scale, equity, fiscal neutrality, and an array of other suggested assignment criteria.[6] Without such empirical input, the criteria remain void of operational content and the resolution of assignment is left to the ebb and flow of political forces alone.

Yet another important dimension is the actual (as opposed to desired)

---

[h]Dollars and employees are actually measures of inputs, *not* outputs, but have often been used as measures of the latter. It should be noted that we could easily spend more without getting any more in the way of output. Also, a dollar spent does not necessarily generate a dollar's worth of benefit.

Table 1-1
Selected Dimensions of the Public Sector: 1960-73

	1960	1973	Percent Change	Average[a] Annual Growth Rate
Expenditures (billions):				
Purchase of goods and services	$ 99.6	$ 276.4	117.5	13.65
Federal	53.5	106.6	99.3	7.64
State-local	46.1	169.8	268.3	20.64
Total expenditures				
Federal	$ 93.0	$ 264.2	184.1	14.16
State-local	49.6	184.4	271.8	20.91
Employment ('000):[b]				
Federal	2,270	2,663	17.3	1.33
State-local	6,083	11,079	82.1	6.32
Total–U.S.	54,234	76,833	41.7	3.21
Gross national product (billions):	$ 503.7	$ 1,294.9	157.1	12.08
Public expenditures as a percent of GNP:				
Total public	28.31	34.64	22.36	1.72
Federal	18.46	20.64	10.51	0.81
State-local	9.85	14.24	44.57	3.43
Employment as a percentage of all employment:				
Total public	15.40	17.88	16.10	1.24
Federal	4.18	3.46	−17.22	−1.33
State-local	11.22	14.42	28.52	2.19

[a]This exceeds the "compound" annual growth rate.

[b]Wage and salary, nonagricultural workers.

Source: *Economic Report of the President* (Washington, D.C.: U.S. Government Printing Office, 1975), tables C-1, C-29, C-68, and C-69.

division of responsibility that has evolved and what it means for each of the levels of government. Separate and distinct from conceptual resolution, if one in fact can be found,[i] is the ad hoc fiscal assignment that blatantly exists and gives rise to very real tensions within the public sector and between the public and private sectors.

Table 1-2 summarizes some data assimilated by Dick Netzer to show how

[i]The situation is further clouded by the ubiquitous trade-off that ultimately *does* make any resolution a political one. We may not be able to have both freedom of choice as political consumer sovereignty and cost savings through economies-of-scale, simultaneously.

Table 1-2
Fiscal Responsibility for Major Urban Services: 1966-67 to 1970-71

| Service | Dollars Spent[a] (Billions) State & Local | | Source of Financing (Percent) | | | | | |
	(1966-67)	(1970-71)	Federal (1966-67)	State (1966-67)	Local (1966-67)	Federal (1970-71)	State (1970-71)	Local (1970-71)
Income distribution								
Welfare	$ 8.2	$12.2	51	35	14	54	35	11
Health and hospitals	6.6	11.2	6	48	46	7	47	46
Housing	1.5	2.6	47	6	47	63	5	32
Public schools	28.1	41.8	7	38	55	10	39	51
Resource allocation								
Police, fire, correction	$ 5.7	$ 9.4	–	21	79	2	22	76
Transportation	2.4	3.7	4	12	84	5	11	84
Water and related	4.3	6.1	2	2	96	8	2	90
Parks and recreation	1.3	2.1	3	4	93	2	5	93
Sanitation	0.9	1.4	–	–	100	–	–	100
Libraries	0.5	0.8	10	10	80	10	13	77
Total, selected services	$59.5	$97.3	13	31	56	18	32	50

[a]By the government actually providing the service.

Sources: Dick Netzer, *Economics and Urban Problems* (New York: Basic Books, 1st ed. 1970 and 2nd ed. 1974), pp. 172 and 228, respectively.

state and local governments meet and finance the three broad collective concerns set forth by Musgrave. What it shows quite clearly is the heavy involvement in urban-related services by local government. Resource-allocation activities ranged from 100 percent locally financed in 1970-71 for sanitation to 76 percent for police. There was very little change in the share of these activities that was locally funded between 1966-67 and 1970-71. What change there has been represents an increased federal involvement in urban problems rather than any greater state commitment. Public services provided to deal with many of the problems of resource allocation remain predominantly locally financed. Public schools is far more of a drain on the local fisc than at any other level. Fifty-one percent of public school expenditures are financed locally, a slight drop from 55 percent in 1966-67. Most of the difference is accounted for by a slightly increased flow of federal funds. Finally, income-distribution activities are heavily funded federally but a large amount remains a local financial responsibility: 11 percent of welfare, 46 percent of health and hospitals, and 32 percent of housing programs. The largest drop has been in housing programs (47 to 32 percent) with welfare coming next (14 to 11 percent).

When one considers that schools and welfare are large components of the local budget and contain substantial redistributive potential, a legitimate question can be raised about whether the burden they exert should remain on the local fisc.[j] Also, the local sector's heavy involvement in the process of urbanization-suburbanization and attendant problems surfaces. It is this involvement, and the financial drain it imposes, that further reinforces the need for urban output measures. If the federal system is to be truly a sharing of power and responsibility, then each of the partners must have a reasonable balance between its needs and its resources. This can best be accomplished with an appropriate allocation of fiscal responsibility which in turn must draw on a set of assignment criteria. These criteria in turn need measures of output for their proper specification.

Measuring Output in the Local Public Sector

Past studies on the output from various governmental units have suffered from two basic flaws: The first is the myopic attention devoted to dollars spent as an indication of what a public unit is providing its citizens. There is a vast literature, often placed under the rubric "determinants" studies, that deals with the question: what are the factors that determine how much a government will spend, either in total or on a specific function?[7] The basic premise can be stated as $E = f(X_1 \ldots X_n)$ where E is dollars spent per capita and $(X_1 \ldots X_n)$ are

[j]Refer to Robert D. Reischauer and Robert W. Hartman, *Reforming School Finance* (Washington, D.C.: Brookings Institution, 1973), Chapter 6; and Committee for Economic Development, *Improving the Public Welfare System* (New York: 1970).

various population, social, governmental, and fiscal variables postulated as correlates of spending levels. Output, however, is measured in dollars and it is assumed that more spending is preferred to less, at least vis-à-vis quantity, quality, or scope of public services provided. While such an approach does uncover factors influencing the level of and variations in expenditures, it does not tell us much of anything about what is made available in the way of outputs or the desirability of the outcomes that a citizen can identify with. As Elinor Ostrom has noted, output is not just a function of dollars spent, either total or per capita:[8] "Far too many articles examining . . . the output of public agencies have utilized . . . input[s] . . . such as total public expenditures or per capita public expenditures." What these studies do, de facto, is use inputs, such as dollars, as proxies for output. Inputs are related to outputs but actual outputs are multidimensional. It is hard to rationalize that the output of a local government is how many dollars it has spent.[k]

Output measurement is also plagued by the "perishable" nature of many of the services provided. These services tend to "disappear," once made available, leaving behind little or no trace of what was actually produced. Quite often there is no physical manifestation to be observed. This leaves the researcher in the troublesome position of measuring a process or an element in a process rather than an end product. The observable facets of such services can often be vague.

It is useful before going on to differentiate several terms that are often used in analysis of public sector operations. Each has a particular meaning that often becomes obfuscated with use.

Output

Output is the amount of a product produced, service rendered, or work done without consideration as to the quality or desirability of what has been done. It is an attempt to determine the "things" that government does in its day-to-day operations. With all of the associated problems, it is the conceptual analog to the loaf of bread or ton of steel produced by the private sector. The word *workload* is also often employed to describe measurable aspects of public output.

Outcome

Outcomes are the consequences that emerge from the outputs of government. While an output is what government does, an outcome is what the citizen gets.[l]

[k]Burkhead gives an excellent discussion of inputs and outputs as elements in the "productive process" for education. Jesse Burkhead, *Input and Output in Large-City High Schools* (Syracuse, New York: Syracuse University Press, 1967), Chapts. 1 and 2.

[l]This distinction is made in Levy, *Urban Outcomes*, pp. 1-23.

Outcomes are the impact of outputs as they relate to a specific goal or objective of public activity. The process of converting private tax dollars into a collective goal is summarized in this flow from tax dollars to goal attainment:

REVENUE →	EXPENDI-	INPUTS →	OUTPUTS →	OUT-	GOAL
(tax dollars)	TURES →	(labor)	(police patrols)	COMES →	ATTAINMENT
	(police de-			(crime	(safety, security)
	partment)			prevention)	

The citizen is most aware of and concerned with the first and last elements in the process, while government's role is to link them as effectively as possible through the four intermediate stages.

Effectiveness

Effectiveness is the extent to which the stated goals and objectives of collective action are being fulfilled.[9] It is a *result*-oriented concept focusing on how nearly perfect the outcome is, *without regard for cost.*[10] Taken literally, it is almost a denial of resource scarcity, priorities, and the basic question of resource utilization. It is focused entirely on the last two elements in the process with no consideration given to the first two.

Efficiency

Efficiency attempts to relate inputs into the public sector to its outputs. It goes one step beyond effectiveness, and asks: how much does it take to get what we want? It is an acknowledgment of the scarcity of resources, priorities, and alternatives.[11] De facto, efficiency is a *process*-oriented concept that scrutinizes how we convert inputs into outputs, but it says nothing about public regard for what is made available. It links the second, third, and fourth elements in the process without giving attention to the remaining elements. As Robert Davis has noted:[12] "... *efficiency* measures the *effectiveness* with which the goal of thrifty use of resources is pursued. ..."

Productivity

Productivity is a measure of efficiency expressed as the ratio of outputs relative to the inputs required to secure that output. It is a measure of the efficiency with which inputs are transformed into outputs.[13] In a sense, productivity is an operationalization of the concept of efficiency.

Performance

Performance is a sort of catch-all term usually employed to indicate "how well we are doing." It can be likened to a *process*-oriented dimension of effectiveness but with attention given to cost considerations. Performance does not mean that we have achieved a stated goal but rather that we are systematically making progress toward it. It links some target or objective that is goal-related to the remaining elements in the chain. Table 1-3 suggests some measures that might be used to reflect the intent of each of the six concepts discussed above.

Approaches to Public Sector Output

For a long time public finance showed virtually no concern whatsoever over public expenditures. The assumption of the "unproductive" nature of government enterprise permeated analysis, and analytical talents were concentrated on how to minimize the burden of taxation. Knut Wicksell was one of the first economists to suggest looking at both sides of the budget (taxes and expenditures)—setting up an array of expenditure alternatives with an array of possible ways to finance them and then voting on the final desired collection.[14] Had this been accomplished, or even if it were feasible, it would establish a quid pro quo in the public realm analagous to costs and benefits in the private sector. While we have moved away from an "unproductivity of public expenditure of funds" stance and developed elaborate conceptual apparatus to account for government intervention, Wicksell's request for a cost-benefit calculus in government decision making remains largely frustrated. One primary reason is a lack of studies measuring those outputs emerging from public operations.

Determinants Studies

One of the more popular approaches to analysis of the state-local sector has focused on dollars spent, usually per capita, often broken down by major expenditure function. It is assumed here that the level of spending and variations across governmental units in expenditures are associated with service levels. While there is an element of truth to that assumption, such orientation does not really get at the core of the output issue for several reasons: First, output is *not* dollars spent. Resolution of crucial output-related issues such as equity in service provision, economies of scale, performance-effectiveness, and functional assignment requires much more information. Second, "Baumol's disease"[15] suggests that the public sector is very susceptible to low productivity and strong inflationary pressure due to relatively high labor inputs. If these assumptions are accurate, then dollars spent will be even less reflective of the real "output" or

Table 1-3
Major Facets of Public-Sector Output Analysis

Urban Function	Output	Outcome	Effectiveness	Efficiency	Performance	Goal
Sanitation	Tons of refuse collected	Cleanliness	Number of complaints	Cost per ton collected	Tons collected per man-day	Improved health and aesthetics
Police	Patrol hours	Security	Dollars lost due to crime	Cost per exposure-hour	Clearance rate	Crime prevention
Fire	Inspections	Fire reduction	Dollars lost due to fire	Cost per inspection	Rate of fires in buildings inspected	Fire prevention
Social services	Cases served	Provision of subsistence needs	Proportion of eligible reached	Cost per case served	Case reduction due to employment	Self-sufficiency
Health and hospital	Admissions	Recovery	Bed utilization	Cost per patient day (by ailment type)	Average length of stay	Better health

service levels and more and more the low productivity-inflation nexus.[m] Finally, there is no extant behavioral theory, like profit maximization in the private sector, underlying the determinants method. It becomes a sort of multiple-regression fishing expedition for statistical correlates.

In 1960 a step was taken by Henry J. Schmandt and G. Ross Stevens to develop a nondollar-based index of the services offered in 19 municipalities.[16] What they did was to break each major function into subfunctions or tasks (some 550 in all), tally the *number* of *different* activities undertaken in each function, and then compare them across governmental units. They found that this proxy for number of tasks was highly correlated with several basic population and governmental dimensions. Whether or not their index is an accurate portrayal of services provided, it does move one step closer to a useful goal—measurement of outputs along multiple dimensions. It acknowledges the fact that output is not dollars and that it becomes manifest in numerous ways.

Bradford, Malt, and Oates

More recently, D.F. Bradford, R.A. Malt, and W.E. Oates (BMO) have focused attention on the difference between the thing(s) that government does in the form of "services directly produced"—(*D* output)—and the thing(s) of "primary interest to the citizen-consumer" (*C* output).[17] A citizen actually is concerned with *C* output but he does not obtain it directly, rather it is obtained through the provision of *D* output by governmental units. Inputs (*I*) can elicit a vast array of outputs (*D*) capable in turn of producing an array of outcomes (*C*). *C* output, as it affects the consumer of public services, is also influenced by other available public and private goods (*Z*) and a broad spectrum of environmental variables (*E*). Thus, we find that the following relationship holds, where *U* is a measure of individual utility:

$$U_i = U(C, Z)$$
$$C_i = C(D, E)$$

which means that individual utility can be stated as follows:

$$U_i = f(D, E, Z)$$

Once again we return to a need for multiple measures of *D* as a first step to determining *C* and then, in conjunction with *E* and *Z*, being able to state something about the impact of government on individual utility. As BMO

---

[m]See the empirical findings on productivity in local government in John P. Ross and Jesse Burkhead, *Productivity in the Local Government Sector* (Lexington, Massachusetts: Lexington Books, D.C. Heath and Co., 1974), Chap. 2.

state:[18] "Even when the distinction between the D- and C-concepts of output is carefully drawn and maintained, a multi-dimensional vector of output remains. . . ." Their model can be diagrammed very simply as follows:

$$I \rightarrow D \rightarrow C$$

but the conversion of I into D and D into C need not be unique. I can lead to numerous patterns of D and we need to choose that D that offers the most desirable set of outcomes (C) from the citizen's perspective. These three elements represent the third, fourth, and fifth steps in the process shown in the previous discussion of "Outcome."

Lancaster's "Characteristics"

Closely related to the approach of BMO is that of Kelvin J. Lancaster, developed as a "new approach to consumer theory." While its purpose is to revise consumer demand theory as it applies to the consumption of private goods, it broaches, conceptually at least, several issues overlapping the domain of public output. Lancaster argues that goods are not consumed *for their own sake* but for the intrinsic properties they embody. Consumers actually seek out the characteristics of goods, these provide them with a certain utility.[n] Goods are just collections of these characteristics. His basic premises are three:[19]

1. A good, per se, does not provide utility, its characteristics do.
2. Goods possess many characteristics but not necessarily uniquely.
3. Goods taken in conjunction can manifest characteristics not found in the goods by themselves.

This approach is readily comparable to the D and C outputs of Bradford, Malt, and Oates; D represents Lancaster's goods and C his characteristics.

While these two approaches are not totally isomorphic, with the D and C outputs of BMO embodying the troublesome conceptual issues of public goods, they are suggestive of a common orientation, that is the multifaceted nature of *all* "goods" as they relate to the utility derived by the final consumer. Table 1-4 is a suggested outline of each approach, showing a public and private good and some attributes that each might manifest.

---

[n]This can be either separately or in conjunction with other goods; a public park combined with efficient transportation may offer more utility than either one by itself.

The Study

The chapters in Part II are an attempt to quantify the "output" and "performance" of the largest municipal government in the United States—New York City, a formidable task of which this represents a first attempt. Output will be measured as those "things that government does or provides" within each of the following five major functional categories: sanitation, health and hospitals, welfare, police, and fire. Performance also is measured, where possible, in an attempt to reflect the effectiveness or productivity of what has been done.[o]

In many instances "ideal" measures are not available and the indexes developed had to be based on those existing sources of information that could be obtained over the time frame chosen—1960-73. The actual measures represent a compromise between the ideal and the practical, based on available sources of data (see Appendix A). Simple indexes of each output activity and performance proxy were computed, relating each year to a base year (usually 1960). As many measures have been presented as felt appropriate to reflect the major activities of each of the five departments under consideration. They are, of course, proxies for municipal output and performance in one of the most complex, diverse, and expensive governmental units in operation anywhere—one, however, that manifests all of the ills that we attribute to urbanism and one that suggests a possible end state of urban evolution.

Table 1-4
Public and Private Goods and Their Attributes

Private

  Good: Meal

  Attributes: nutrition   aesthetics   taste   social setting   environment   convenience

Public

  Good: Police protection

  Attributes:[a] patrols (foot and vehicular)   emergency service   surveillance   crime investigation   recovery of stolen property   seizure of contraband   apprehension of criminals

---

Note: Good is used here as it is most closely identified with what the consumer pays for: dollars for a meal and taxes for police protection.

[a]In the case of a public good each of these might have attributes that are of a more primal nature to the consumer, for example, patrols may produce security and reduce fear and anxiety.

---

[o]*Performance* will be used here as a sort of catch-all for the many nonoutput facets of municipal operations. The word *activity* will be used interchangeably with output.

Notes

1. U.S. Bureau of the Census, *Census of Government: 1972*, vol. 4, *Government Finances* (Washington, D.C.: U.S. Government Printing Office, 1973), table 1.

2. Robert L. Bish, *The Public Economy of Metropolitan Areas* (Chicago: Markham, 1971).

3. Donald Phares, *State-Local Tax Equity* (Lexington, Massachusetts: Lexington Books, D.C. Heath and Co., 1973), chap. 2.

4. Richard Musgrave, *The Theory of Public Finance* (New York: McGraw-Hill, 1959).

5. Alan K. Campbell, "Most Dynamic Sector," *National Civic Review*, vol. 52 (February 1964), pp. 74-82.

6. Donald Phares, "Assignment of Functions: An Economic Framework," in *Governmental Functions and Processes: Local and Areawide* (Washington, D.C.: Advisory Commission on Intergovernmental Relations, 1974), pp. 119-41.

7. Roy W. Bahl, "Studies on Determinants of Public Expenditures: A Review," in Selma Mushkin and John F. Cotton, eds., *Functional Federalism* (Washington, D.C.: State and Local Finances Project, The George Washington University, 1968), pp. 184-207.

8. Elinor Ostrom, "The Need for Multiple Indicators in Measuring the Output of Public Agencies," in Frank P. Scioli, Jr. and Thomas J. Cook, eds., *Methodologies for Analyzing Public Policy* (Lexington, Massachusetts: Lexington Books, D.C. Heath and Co., 1975), p. 15.

9. The Urban Institute and ICMA, *Measuring the Effectiveness of Basic Municipal Services* (Washington, D.C.: The Urban Institute, February 1974), p. 3.

10. Robert Davis, "Measuring Effectiveness of Municipal Services," *Management Information Service*, ICMA, vol. 2 (August 1970), p. 4.

11. Ibid.

12. Ibid.

13. John P. Ross and Jesse Burkhead, *Productivity in the Local Government Sector* (Lexington, Massachusetts: Lexington Books, D.C. Heath and Co., 1974), chap. 2.

14. Knut Wicksell, "A New Principle of Just Taxation," in R.A. Musgrave and A. Peacock, eds., *Classics in the Theory of Public Finance* (New York: MacMillan, 1958), pp. 72-118.

15. William J. Baumol, "Macroeconomics of Unbalanced Growth: The Anatomy of Urban Crisis," *American Economic Review*, vol. 57 (June 1967), pp. 415-26.

16. Henry J. Schmandt and G. Ross Stevens, "Measuring Municipal Output," *National Tax Journal*, vol. 13 (December 1960), pp. 369-75.

17. D.F. Bradford, R.A. Malt, and W.E. Oates, "The Rising Cost of Local

Public Services: Some Evidence and Reflections," *National Tax Journal*, vol. 22 (June 1969), p. 186.

18. Ibid., p. 188.

19. Kelvin J. Lancaster, "A New Approach to Consumer Theory," *Journal of Political Economy*, vol. 74 (April 1966), p. 134.

2
Perspective on New York City

The goal of this study is to document the evolution in public service offerings in New York City, looking in detail at the various facets that comprise a department's activities rather than simply dollars expended or people employed. Before considering these findings in Chapters 3-7, it is useful to set some perspective on the city's current status and why it warrants our attention.

To begin, one can examine certain features of the population of New York and see how they have evolved over time; selected data on such characteristics are presented in Table 2-1. While none is an unequivocal determinant of municipal output, each is definitely related in a contextual sense and serves to define the milieu in which shifts in service provision occurred.

Shifts in the City's Population Makeup

Over the decade 1960-70, total population grew very little. There were about 7.9 million people living in New York in 1970, just slightly more than 1 percent above 1960. Up to this point population had continued to rise, albeit not by much. By 1973, however, it had begun to fall, dropping to 7.7 million, a decline of over 2 percent in just three years. The impact of decentralization, which had slowed growth to nearly zero between 1960 and 1970 now elicited an absolute drop in population of almost 170,000. Within this overall change, certain components showed even greater fluctuation.

The "dependent"[a] population under 18, for example, had grown more rapidly than total population until 1970 but then declined faster up to 1973. By then this group was at about the same level as in 1960. "Dependent" population over 65, on the other hand, rose sharply during the decade 1960-70 (16.5%) and then continued upward slightly after 1970. Those persons falling between 18 and 65 decreased over this entire time span. Thus, the age groups tending to be more dependent on municipal services—the young and the elderly—have generally grown in size relative to those considered to be in their "productive" years, rising from 38 percent to 40 percent of the city's population.

There has been an even more dramatic shift in the racial makeup of the city than in its age composition. New York population grew almost 54 percent in the

---

[a]Population under 18 and over 65 are often viewed as dependent in that they are not a part of the productive labor force and use more in the way of public services, such as education and health care.

19

Table 2-1
New York City Population Characteristics: 1960-73

Category	1960	1970	1973	% Change 1960-70	% Change 1970-73
Total population	7,783,314	7,894,798	7,717,000	1.4	−2.3
Population under 18	2,164,527	2,234,819	2,134,000	3.2	−4.5
Population 18-65	4,803,630	4,712,164	4,538,000	−1.9	−3.7
Population 65 and over	813,827	947,878	986,000	16.5	2.3
Black population	1,084,862	1,665,470	1,755,180[a]	53.5	5.4
Hispanic population	n.a	1,112,868	1,241,200	n.a.	11.5
Families with female heads	268,625	354,735	431,000	32.1	21.5

Note: n.a. = not available.

[a]Estimated as 90 percent of reported nonwhite population.

Sources: U.S. Bureau of the Census, *Characteristics of the Population*, vol. 1, pt. 34, New York 1960 and 1970; and Blanche Bernstein and Arley Bondarin, *New York City Population–1973* (New York: Center for New York City Affairs, New School for Social Research, 1974).

decade 1960-70 and then by another 5 percent in the following three years. Black population grew from 14 percent to 23 percent of total population over this period while the Hispanic population also rose sharply, more than 11 percent between 1970 and 1973.[b] This group now comprises 16 percent of the population. It is clear that minority groups within the city are increasing rapidly while the white population is decreasing. In relative terms, minorities now account for 39 percent of New York's residents. In general, minorities in central cities manifest an above-average incidence of poverty[c] and require more in the way of direct poverty linked services such as welfare, special education, and health and social services. A high incidence of poverty also exerts added pressure for police and fire services and creates a need for more frequent refuse removal.

Another population group generally found to be "poverty prone" is families with a female head. This category has also shown a sharp increase. Between 1960 and 1970, female-headed families rose more than 32 percent and in the following three years increased an additional 21.5 percent. Each of these major trends implies that greater demands for city services—particularly those that are poverty related—could be anticipated for the years under examination.

While the resident populace is the major factor influencing public service output, a large transient population also exerts its pressure on the New York fisc. This group is of considerably more significance in New York than in other

[b]Data for 1960 are not available on this group but there were significant increases between 1960 and 1970 as well.

[c]See Blanche Berstein and Arley Bondarin, "Income Distribution in New York City," *City Almanac*, vol. 9 (April 1975), for data on income trends in New York broken down by race.

cities due to its status as a commercial, financial, tourist, and international center as well as one of the major employment foci in the Northeast. While many people visit New York only on an irregular basis, a large number of workers commute in and out of the city daily and place additional demands on various city departments on a regular basis. New York City employed about 3.74 million people in 1970, 6 percent more than in 1960. But by 1973 it had fallen back to the 1960 level.[1] Not all these workers live outside city limits (although large numbers do) but a large volume of commuting workers and visitors do require services, especially those related to public safety and transportation for which quid pro quo may not be received.[d]

Scale of Municipal Operations: Employment and Expenditures

In terms of dollars spent and people provided with jobs, the city of New York has grown very significantly in the period 1960-73; this is shown clearly in Table 2-2. City employment has risen from 247,000 to 380,000 during this 13-year period, some 54 percent. Shifting attention to dollars, the budget for the city has grown steadily from $2.4 to $10.2 billion during the same period; this is a 321 percent increase. Considering the decline in population, the impact of such budget expansion looms even more dominant. On a per-capita basis, expenses have risen from $311 in 1960 to a whopping $1,304 in 1973-74.[2] This represents growth of 319 percent over thirteen years or an average of about 25 percent *per year*. As a claim on personal income, the impact of this growing municipal activity is equally as pronounced. The expense budget as a percentage of personal income has manifest a constant upward trend from 11.8 percent in 1963-64 to 20.3 percent in 1973-74, thus nearly doubling in ten years.[3]

When one disaggregates public activity along functional lines, similar trends are uncovered but the variance is much greater as shown in Table 2-2. Police manpower rose 13,000 (50%) and expenditures $380 million (170%); fire manpower rose over 3,000 (27%) and expenditures $163 million (148%). Sanitation employment went up the least (6%) as did hospitals up until 1970. Expenditures, however, continued to grow, $163 (161%) and $431 million (312%), respectively. Both of these functions were eventually incorporated into larger agencies, which accounts for a part of the budget rise. After 1970 hospital employment jumped some 22 percent to an all-time high. The largest growth in any city department was that experienced by social services—employment rose 210 percent between 1960 and 1970 and then another 27 percent between 1970 and 1973. This is clearly associated with the population trends mentioned

[d]The issue of exploitation of the central city by surrounding suburbs is not addressed here, but just mentioned as a possibility. Whatever the case vis-à-vis compensation, one can hardly argue with the direction of the pressure that commuters exert on central-city service levels.

Table 2-2
New York City Employment and Expenditures by Function: 1960-73

Function[a]	Employment					Expenditures (Millions)		
	1960[b]	1970[b]	1973[c]	% Change 1960-70	% Change 1970-73	1960-61	1973-74	% Change 1960-61 to 1973-74
Total	246,812	371,094	380,327[d]	50	2	$2,419	$10,172	321
Police	26,106	36,856	39,791	41	8	223	603	170
Fire	11,863	14,865	15,109	25	2	110	273	148
Sanitation	13,442	14,192	14,285	6	1	97[e]	253[e]	161
Hospitals	37,497	37,438	45,594[f]	g	22	138[h]	569[h]	312
Social services	8,317	25,762	32,575	210	27	350	2,684	667

[a]Exclusive of education. The numbers represent each function as best as possible.

[b]Employment figures are as of December 31st of the previous year.

[c]Employment figures are modified budget figures for fiscal year 1973-74.

[d]Full-time equivalent, taken from Bureau of the Census, *Local Government Employment in Selected Metropolitan Areas and Large Counties* (Washington, D.C.: U.S. Government Printing Office, GE73, no. 3, November 1974).

[e]Reflects establishment of Environmental Protection Administration in 1968.

[f]Taken from "New York City Finances: A Ten Year Review," *Real Estate News*, vol. 55 (June-July 1974), p. 20.

[g]Less than 1 percent.

[h]Reflects evolution of Department of Hospitals into Health and Hospital Corporation in 1970.

Sources: City of New York, Department of Personnel, Civil Service Commission, *Annual Report* (New York: 1959 and 1969); City of New York, *Schedule Supporting the Executive Budget for 1974-75* (New York: no date); *Annual Report of the Comptroller of the City of New York,* fiscal years 1960-61 to 1973-74.

earlier. Social services now provides employment for 32,575 persons. Dollars expended for social services literally exploded between 1960-61 and 1973-74, rising from $350 to $2,684 million, an increase in excess of 660 percent.

Every one of the departments examined has undergone growth in employment and expenditures, usually of major proportions. On a per-capita basis and as a percentage of personal income, the upward drift in city activity has been steady and increasingly more burdensome. As a benchmark, one can consider the following: In 1971-72 all local governments spent $118 billion, $43.6 billion of which was disbursed by some 19,000 municipalities. New York City alone accounted for $9.6 billion or nearly 22 percent of all municipal- and 8 percent of all local-government expenditures in the United States.[4]

Certain other expenditure trends are also of consequence[5] and should be noted even though they are not explicitly considered in the later chapters.[e] The budget for education rose 218 percent from $870 to $2,769 million between 1963-64 and 1973-74; employment climbed at the same time from 60,196 to 93,034, more than 50 percent. The cost of debt service had reached $868 million by 1973-74 compared with $339 million in 1963-64—this on a level of gross funded debt that rose from $4.5 to $6.9 billion. The cost of servicing this debt rose by 155 percent while the volume of debt went up a little over 50 percent; debt service has become one of the major items in the city's budget. A final area of rapidly rising fiscal impact is the city's contribution to various pension plans. These claims have increased from $311 million in 1963-64 to $933 million in 1973-74, over 200 percent. It has been projected that the cost of pension contributions could conceivably reach $2 billion per year by 1980,[6] especially if properly funded.

These expenditure trends have also become manifest in the earnings of city employees. As Table 2-3 shows clearly, *every* department's average-wage level has risen in excess of 50 percent over the period 1965-72. Certain job categories within these department have experienced even greater relative advances. It should be noted that both salaries and wages and the more inclusive category of personnel cost have not risen as a percentage of the total budget as the wage data might lead one to believe. In fact, salaries and wages have actually fallen ten points to 39 percent of the budget while total personnel costs have dropped from 60 to 47 percent; both are significant declines. New pressure on the New York fisc has come from an increased role for social and medical care (5 to 14%) and public-assistance payments (8 to 12%).[7] Also, while wages are high in New York, other cities do have more generous pay scales for their police, fire, and teaching staff.[8]

Yet another way to set New York's operations in focus is to compare its

---

[e]The force of these trends has an impact on the "competitive" status of any department to expand its budget. One case in point is education, which has always been the primary claim on New York's fisc. The explosive growth in social services, however, is rapidly moving it to a primary status.

Table 2-3
Average Wages by Department: 1965 and 1972

Department[a]	1965	1972	% Change 1965-72
Police	$8,685	$14,489	66.8
Fire	8,603	15,966	85.6
Sanitation	7,421	12,678	70.8
Health & Hospital	6,065	9,661	59.3
Social Services	5,796	9,275	60.0

[a]Annual averages are shown for the "uniformed" personnel in police, fire, and sanitation and "overall" averages in health and hospital and social services.
Source: Roy W. Bahl, Alan K. Campbell, and David Greytak, *Taxes, Expenditures, and the Economic Base: Case Study of New York City* (New York: Praeger Publishers, 1975), tables 3.A.1-3.A.17.

per-capita expenditures to those in the ten largest United States cities.[9] Such comparisons help to underscore the nature of the difference between New York City and the rest of urban America (refer to Table 2-4). For every one of the expenditure categories shown, New York is well above the average for the "ten-largest," often by a factor exceeding two to one. The range is from a low of 114 percent for police and 117 percent for fire to a high of 226 percent on education, 249 percent on welfare, and 210 percent on health and hospitals. It is interesting to note those categories exceeding 200 percent of the ten-city average are all "variable" functions. These are responsibilities *not* usually assumed by municipal government. "Common"[f] functions do exceed the average but not by nearly as much. This points to the considerably broader scope of municipal operations in New York City. Growth in the role of variable operations is also evident: the index relative to the ten-city average has risen from 165 to 201 between 1966 and 1971, while common functions have dropped from 117 to 112.

No matter where one looks, the financial picture of New York over the period 1960-73 is one of rapid relative and absolute expansion. Quite often growth has assumed staggering proportions and become manifest in tens-of-thousands of new jobs, a plethora of new programs, and improved quantity, quality, and scope for those already in operation.

Fiscal Sketch of New York: How the
Bills Get Paid

Underlying the many changes in employment and expenditures just outlined is the fiscal side of New York's operations. The tensions inherent in financing such

[f]Those usually provided by municipal government.

Table 2-4

Per-capita Expenditures in the Ten Largest United States Cities Compared with New York: 1971

Expenditure Category	New York	10-City Average[a]	Index of New York to 10-City Average
Total	$1,207	$685	176
Interest on debt[b]	31	19	163
Retirement[b]	78	42	186
Personal service[b]	477	296	161
Police[c]	65	57	114
Fire[c]	28	24	117
Sanitation[c]	42	34	124
Education[d]	253	112	226
Health & hospital[d]	128	61	210
Welfare[d]	254	102	249
Variable functions[d]			
(1971)	989	491	201
(1966)	445	270	112
Common Functions[c]			
(1971)	218	194	112
(1966)	138	118	117

Note: The cities are Chicago, Los Angeles, Philadelphia, Detroit, Houston, Baltimore, Dallas, Washington, Cleveland, and New York.

[a]This is a weighted average: total expenditures divided by total population for all ten cities, including New York.

[b]"Object" categories.

[c]"Common" functions, usually a municipal responsibility.

[d]"Variable" functions, not usually a municipal responsibility.

Source: Roy W. Bahl, Alan K. Campbell, and David Greytak, *Taxes, Expenditures, and the Economic Base: Case Study of New York City* (New York: Praeger Publishers, 1975), tables 3.3-3.6.

a scale of municipal endeavor have become manifest as several pronounced shifts in those primary fiscal variables shown in Tables 2-5 and 2-6. To cope with the more than tripling of expenditures in the ten years between 1963-64 and 1973-74, revenues have had to expand along every possible fiscal front.

Of the more than $7 billion growth in spending, some $3,958 billion (57%) was derived from a larger flow of state and federal aid into the city. Over the decade shown state aid expanded 357 percent while federal aid rose by 983 percent. As Table 2-6 documents, this has led to a much larger relative share of health services being absorbed by the state and federal governments. This is not the case with income transfers, however, which have gone from being 27 to 29 percent locally financed. Education has accounted for the great bulk of the

Table 2-5
Major Revenue Sources for New York City: 1963-64 to 1973-74 (Millions)

Year[a]	Total Revenue	Intergovernmental Aid		Local Revenue Sources					
		State	Federal	Total Taxes	Real Estate Taxes	Sales-Use Taxes	Business Taxes	Personal Income Taxes	All Other
1963-64	$ 3,124	$ 605	$ 183	$2,337	$1,220	$421	$224	$ (c)	$ 471
(% of total)[b]	(100)	(19)	(6)	(75)	(39)	(13)	(7)	(c)	(15)
1965-66	3,894	1,011	308	2,576	1,409	384	244	(c)	537
(% of total)	(100)	(26)	(8)	(66)	(36)	(10)	(6)	(c)	(14)
1967-68	5,272	1,467	746	3,059	1,648	413	310	170	518
(% of total)	(100)	(28)	(14)	(58)	(31)	(8)	(6)	(3)	(10)
1969-70	6,591	1,993	1,060	3,538	1,831	467	320	205	715
(% of total)	(100)	(30)	(16)	(54)	(28)	(7)	(5)	(3)	(11)
1971-72	8,651	2,517	1,524	4,610	2,100	520	429	443	1,117
(% of total)	(100)	(29)	(18)	(53)	(24)	(6)	(5)	(5)	(13)
1973-74	10,160	2,765	1,981	5,414	2,655	594	515	557	1,094
(% of total)	(100)	(27)	(19)	(53)	(26)	(6)	(6)	(5)	(11)
10-year change									
Increase	$ 7,036	$2,160	$1,798	$3,077	$1,435	$173	$291	$557[d]	$ 623
(% of total)	(100)	(31)	(26)	(44)	(20)	(2)	(4)	(8)	(9)
Percent increase	225	357	983	132	118	41	130	228[d]	132
Average annual increase	22.5%	35.7%	98.3%	13.2%	11.8%	4.1%	13.0%	22.8%	13.2%

aSelected years.
bEach revenue source as a percent of total revenue.
cNo tax in effect.
dFrom 1967-68 to 1973-74.

Source: Derived from data contained in The New York Chamber of Commerce and Industry, "New York City Finances: A Ten Year Review—1963-64, 1973-74," *Real Estate News*, vol. 55 (June-July 1974), pp. 16-20.

Table 2-6
Source of City Revenue by Function and Level of Government: 1960-61 to 1970-71

		Functional Category[a]		
			Human-resource Development	
Revenue Distribution[b]	Total Budget	Public Safety[c]	Income Transfers	Health Services
1960-61				
Local	80	100	27	85
State	15	d	30	13
Federal	5	d	43	2
Dollars expended (millions)	$2,425	$370	$ 236	$ 256
1970-71				
Local	62	99	29	39
State	22	d	29	28
Federal	17	d	42	33
Dollars expended (millions)	$7,828	$958	$1,368	$1,213
Change[e]				
Local	–18	–1	+2	–46
State	+7	0	–1	+15
Federal	+12	0	–1	+31
Dollars expended (millions)	$5,403	$588	$1,132	$ 957

[a]Sanitation is not shown but it is entirely locally financed.

[b]Percent of revenue for each function derived from each level of government.

[c]Police and fire services.

[d]Less than 0.5 percent.

[e]Amount in 1970-71 minus that in 1960-61.

Source: Derived from data contained in Charles Brecher, *Where Have All the Dollars Gone?* (New York: Praeger Publishers, 1974), tables 2.2 and 2.4.

remaining relative realignment. The net result of these new aid flows has been that the city budget has moved from a local-state-federal sharing of 75-19-6 percent to 53-27-19 percent over a decade. Intergovernmental aid has become the largest single revenue source for New York City, now nearly matching the 53 percent of the budget financed locally. The trend in aid, however, appears to have taken a reversal of late. Federal aid has fallen from its peak of 22 percent of revenue in 1972-73 to 19 percent as of 1973-74. Dollars of aid received have actually fallen in spite of the injection of revenue-sharing funds. Question is also being raised concerning New York State's capacity to expand any further its financial commitment to New York City.[g] It seems unlikely that the aid trends of the past decade can be maintained to keep pace with growth in expenditures. The cost will increasingly have to fall on local resources, already extremely burdened under the heavy load.

At the local level, the fiscal mainstay is the real-estate tax, which accounts for 26 percent of total revenue or about one-half of locally raised revenue. This tax has paid for about 20 percent of the $7 billion in new spending over the decade. To accomplish this the tax rate has been raised from $4.41 per $100 of assessed valuation in 1964 to $8.19 in 1975. The high rate of taxation has elicited a delinquency rate that is the highest since the Depression, $220 million in fiscal 1975.[10] Of major importance is the city income tax put into effect in fiscal 1967-68. Currently it raises nearly $600 million, 5 percent of all revenue. It has absorbed 8 percent of the expansion in spending between 1963-64 and 1973-74. Next come the sales-use and business taxes; each accounted for another 5 percent of total revenue but has not contributed a great deal to the budget expansion.

Finally, there is the "all other" category, which has become second largest to the property tax and has paid 9 percent of the new costs. The problem here is that this $1 billion-plus category contains a great many lesser revenue instruments that have been enacted to "squeeze out additional dollars." Their existence attests to the crisis nature of fiscal decision making in New York and a constant attempt to keep pace with a rapidly growing budget.[11] They have often been characterized as a nuisance.

Examination of the various sources of revenue serves to underscore the pressure that has been placed on each to raise *an additional* $7 billion in ten years. When one converts this into the impact on an average taxpayer, the pressure emerges as even more severe. During the period 1971-74, taxes (federal, state, and local) claimed 32 cents of every additional dollar of income for lower income families, 43 cents at the moderate level and 49 cents at the higher income level. It has been speculated that "the total direct and indirect tax bill of a family [in the New York region] . . . could be as much as half of income."[12]

New York as the Epitome of Urbanization

To obtain an appropriate perspective on the output of municipal services in New York City one final factor should be mentioned. It is that this city represents the most advanced "state of urbanization" in the United States, at a scale that far surpasses anything in existence elsewhere.[h] As such, it can be stated that New York epitomizes one possible end state of urban development, with all the

[g]Refer to the many articles on New York State's fiscal status in the *New York Times* or *Wall Street Journal* during the months August to December, 1975.

[h]Consider just the following few dimensions: a population of 7.8 million, personal income in excess of $50 billion, and municipal spending of $12 billion.

associated problems. Such an advanced state of urban evolution places demands on "collective action" to cope with the many issues that arise out of unconstrained, uncoordinated private activity. These demands become converted into a pressure for government, in this case the City of New York, to "ameliorate a condition, solve a problem, or deal with a crisis." The greater the incidence of undesired conditions, problems, or crises, the greater the pressure on government to "do something."

Economists have long recognized the potential for certain private behavior to "spill over" onto others not directly involved in the original act—"externalities."[13] Certain forms of consumption, such as an excessive ingestion of alcohol or drugs, can turn an individually harmless person and automobile into a lethal combination. Overt criminal acts are in their very essence meant to have an impact on someone else. Production behavior, such as the polluting firm, can also create an undesirable situation for "others." The point of each example is that those affected have no recourse to the harm or loss-inducing agent except through collective action, usually government.

When large numbers of persons are focused in a relatively small land area, the existence of externalities such as pollution, crime, and congestion looms even more ominous. The sheer concentration of persons, business, and economic activity in a city such as New York makes it a place where externalities of all types abound, of a nature and severity not encountered elsewhere.

One other factor exerts unusual pressure on the resources of New York's government. Central cities have increasingly become the focus of large dependent populations—minorities, aged, poor, children. The unmet needs of these people, for food, housing, and medical attention, often become the responsibility of society—all of this in the context of a shrinking tax base.[i] This is the case in New York with more than 1 million persons on welfare and additional hundreds of thousands requiring other social and health services. The city expends billions of dollars every year on social and health programs, housing, and the like to meet the needs of its large indigent populace. While part of the cost is borne by the state and federal governments, a large chunk remains a local fiscal drain. In many respects central cities, New York especially, have taken on the appearance of reservations, with local government forced into the role of keeper.[14]

Each of these factors exerts a strong upward force on public service levels in any city. But when the nature and severity of the situation assumes the stature of that in New York the pressure is even greater. The following five chapters examine in detail just how these forces have become manifest as increased levels of public services.

Notes

1. George Roniger, "The Economy of the New York Region," *City Almanac*, vol. 10 (June 1975), p. 14, table 12.

---

iThis can be either absolute or relative to an expanding base of needs.

2. New York Chamber of Commerce and Industry, "New York City Finances: A Ten Year Review—1963-64, 1973-74," *Real Estate News*, vol. 55 (June-July 1974), table I.

3. Ibid., table II.

4. Bureau of the Census, *Census of Governments: 1972*, vol. 4, *Government Finances* (Washington, D.C.: U.S. Government Printing Office, 1973), tables 1 and 53.

5. Taken from New York Chamber of Commerce and Industry, "New York City Finances."

6. "How to Save New York," *Time* (October 20, 1975), p. 15.

7. Derived from Charles Brecher, *Where Have All the Dollars Gone?* (New York: Praeger Publishers, 1974), table 1.5.

8. "New York's Last Gasp," *Newsweek* (August 4, 1975), p. 25.

9. Data are taken from Roy W. Bahl, Alan K. Campbell, and David Greytak, *Taxes, Expenditures, and the Economic Base: Case Study of New York City* (New York: Praeger Publishers, 1974), pp. 163-74.

10. See Steven R. Weisman, "How New York Became a Fiscal Junkie," *The New York Times Magazine* (August 17, 1975), pp. 8 *et passim*, and "How to Save New York," p. 16.

11. Weisman, "How New York Became a Fiscal Junkie."

12. "How High Can Taxes Go?" *New York Times* (June 1, 1975), sect. IV, p. 1, or for more detail, Roy Bahl et al. "Comparative Tax Burdens in Manhattan, Queens and Selected New York Metropolitan Area Suburbs," Occasional Paper No. 20, Metropolitan Studies Program, Syracuse University, June 1975.

13. See E.J. Mishan, "The Postwar Literature on Externalities: An Interpretive Essay," *Journal of Economic Literature*, vol. 9 (March 1971), pp. 1-28.

14. Norton Long, "The City as Reservation," *Public Interest*, no. 25 (Fall 1971), pp. 22-38.

Part II:
Analysis of Municipal
Services in New York City

3

Police Department

Overview

The primary mission of the New York City Police Department (NYPD) is to provide protection for persons and property through the prevention and control of crime, to provide assistance to other government bodies in the performance of their duties, and to assist distressed private individuals. Secondary objectives are to identify, locate, and apprehend suspected and known criminals; to facilitate vehicular and pedestrian traffic; and to assist in emergency rescue situations. These functions are supported by facilities and equipment maintenance, training, and administrative and technical services.[1] In all, the accomplishment of these many and diverse activities occupied a uniformed force in excess of 30,000 and an additional 7,000 civilian personnel operating out of 77 station houses in 1970. These numbers, however, greatly understate the overall impact of what is referred to as "police work." Indeed, if the combined forces of the Transit Police (2,400) and the Housing Police (1,200) were to be included as part of the city's protective force, NYPD would still account for 90 percent of the total.[2]

Police work is usually considered a dangerous occupation and it appears that it is increasingly so. Line-of-duty injuries rose by 147 percent, line-of-duty deaths by 83 percent, and man-days lost due to injuries by 110 percent between 1963 and 1970.[3] Since the growth of injuries and deaths far exceeds that of manpower (25%) and exposure (34%), it appears that working for NYPD is a more and more hazardous occupation. In 1970, 3,666 injuries and twelve deaths occurred in the line of duty, with an average of one month lost per injury. Of all injuries, 1,182 were the result of assaults on police officers with an average of 54 days lost per incident.

The task at hand is to consider changes in police department operations between 1960 and 1973. As noted earlier, the incredibly varied nature and scope of services performed by all New York City departments makes performance evaluation an elusive endeavor. Indeed, just a definition of service and performance is complex in itself; this is complicated further when one must cope with data that have not been assimilated with this purpose in mind. A major problem with quantification is that there is often no tangible product to be counted, unlike the case when one is considering output of, for example, manufactured goods.[a] In considering police output, we are dealing with nebulous public

---

[a]Discussion of the concepts and difficulties involved in measuring public service output can be found in John P. Ross and Jesse Burkhead, *Productivity in the Local Government Sector* (Lexington, Massachusetts: Lexington Books, D.C. Heath and Co., 1974).

concerns and concepts such as "public safety, protection, law and order," all of which are nonmeasurable, nonoperational variables. It is only possible to quantify those activities undertaken by the police department *in an attempt to achieve* a desired state of "safety" or "order."

The New York Police Department represents a particular challenge in defining activities in terms of available statistics because of the number of departmental responsibilities. Police department activities can be divided into two main types: primary and supportive. The major primary activities—patrol, crime investigation, and arrest—are widely acknowledged as "police work," as are traffic control and emergency service. However, there are lesser known primary activities, which are performed by specialized units within NYPD. One such unit is the Harbor Precinct, which is responsible for crime control, marine traffic functions, and search and rescue operations in the bodies of water around the city. Similar duties are performed in the air by the Aviation Unit. The Missing Persons Unit has the specialized task of locating persons reported missing and identifying the unidentified sick or dead. Another specialized unit is the Bomb Squad, which responds to calls regarding real or suspected bombs, and searches for, removes, or defuses explosive devices. Growth in measurable aspects of these activities is discussed in greater detail below.

In addition to responsibilities directly affecting the citizenry, the police are often called upon to assist other departments, such as by diverting traffic at the scene of a fire. In 1970 police assisted the fire department in 441 incidents, while assistance to other departments (e.g., placing police barriers; removal of sick, injured, or dead person) totaled 2,134 incidents. The NYPD must also provide extra protection to visiting dignitaries and heads of state. A recent example is the November 1974 visit to the General Assembly of the United Nations by Yasir Arafat. More than 150 New York City policemen were on hand for the arrival of his ariplane while 200 policemen surrounded his hotel during a demonstration.[4] This is not the full extent of extra protection provided during the visit, but is indicative of the magnitude of demands such incidents exert.

As mentioned earlier, the category "supportive activities" includes operations that expedite the performance of primary functions; these include fingerprinting, photography, and ballistics and laboratory procedures. Also within this category are activities common to all organizations, such as secretarial, clerical, and other administrative functions; these include training of police recruits; storage and distribution of supplies and materials; and janitorial and maintenance service. Data on these generalized types of activities are not available, with the exception of those of the police medical unit. Supportive activities within the exclusive domain of the police department include: arrest processing (booking); interrogation of suspects; court appearances; storage, classification and distribution of lost and stolen property; and issuance of some licenses and permits.

The above discussion includes major activities of NYPD and is indicative of their diversity; other lesser activities and responsibilities have been omitted. It should be emphasized that, while the average patrolman is called upon to perform many primary and supportive activities, a wide variety of specialized personnel is exclusively concerned with many of these specialized functions.

Shifting focus to an analysis of NYPD, two difficulties are encountered: First, the diverse nature of the activities performed makes it impossible to combine them into a composite index. Second, not all activities are quantifiable. Therefore, our approach will be to focus on those quantifiable traits that best proxy the essence of the primary and supportive services of NYPD.

Difficulties of measurement are perhaps best illustrated in the area of crime prevention. Many people would readily agree that crime prevention is the single most important activity of a police department. However, there is simply no way to determine the number of crimes that have been prevented. Other measurable activities can be taken as indicators of crime prevention but only imperfectly so. As examples, patrol duty is meant to deter crime by the visible presence of the police,[b] while arrest and subsequent detention of those considered to have committed a crime are methods of cutting down further (potential) crime. Thus, these two statistics can be subjected to dual interpretation. While representing definite measures of activity, they also seem to at least overlap the realm of performance indicators for crime prevention.

Certain other indicators also represent a compromise between those measures desired and those available. For example, crimes recorded in a given year are considered a proxy measure for investigation, rather than simply a reflection of crime trends. It should not be assumed that the crimes reported in the NYPD *Annual Report* represent all crimes committed. It is widely recognized that a large volume of crime never gets reported (not only in New York, but throughout the United States).[c] This problem does not affect the investigation of reported crimes, but does suggest that many more crimes could be dealt with than is currently the case. Other problems can be noted regarding the crime-reporting system used by local police departments—that ultimately becomes reflected in the FBI's Uniform Crime Report—such as the method for crime classification.[d] While questions of classification and the recording of crime may

[b]James Q. Wilson has raised some doubts concerning this assumption see "Do the Police Prevent Crime?" *New York Times Magazine* (October 6, 1974), p. 18 *et passim.*

[c]The problem of underreporting is discussed more thoroughly in the President's Commission on Law Enforcement and Administration of Justice, *The Challenge of Crime in a Free Society* (Washington, D.C.: U.S. Government Printing Office, 1967), pp. 20-21; see Ramsey Clark, *Crime in America* (New York: Simon and Schuster, 1970), pp. 44-55 for a discussion of underreporting and the Uniform Crime Reports. More recent national surveys regarding the extent of disparity between "officially" reported crime and actual crime incidents are noted in *New York Times*, January 27, 1974, p. 1. These surveys indicate that reported rapes, robberies, and assaults, for example, represent approximately half of actual crime in these categories.

[d]See, for example, Albert J. Reiss, Jr., "Assessing the Current Crime Wave," *Crime in Urban Society*, ed. Barbara N. McTenan (New York: Dunellen Publishing Company, 1970), p. 27. An excellent review of the crime data problem can be found in *Report on National Needs for Criminal Justice Statistics* (Washington, D.C.: Governments Division, Bureau of the Census, August 1968).

prove to be serious problems in any analysis of crime trends, they do not offer the same drawbacks for our analysis of police activity. We assume that all crimes recorded by the police are investigated (to some degree), regardless of what category they are recorded under.

Nonetheless, it should not be assumed that the police exert no influence over the number of crimes reported during any given period. Obviously, every actual crime reported by a citizen will be recorded and investigated. However, some (unknown) portion of total crime is discovered and reported exclusively by members of the police department. Pressure from the public, departmental leadership, or political sources might lead to a greater reporting of specific types of crime due to, for example, a drive against muggings or a campaign to "clean up Times Square." There may or may not be a decrease in crime recorded in other categories as special efforts are concentrated on one type of crime or one specific locality. Police attitude can also affect the recorded number of some types of offenses that are not widely viewed as criminal or do not generate much in the way of public attention. Crimes that entail only behavior or testimony, without physical evidence, are strongly affected by the attitude of the police department in seeking out and reporting such crimes.[5] One example might be unlicensed peddling. If the officer on patrol does not issue a summons to the peddler, then no crime is reported even though technically there has been a violation. The amount of police activity in crimes of this sort, (which covers most "victimless" crimes), is thus influenced by the department as a whole and by the attitude of individual officers.

Along with the lack of ideal measures for police activity and performance, certain caveats must be stated about those that are available. Before analyzing the statistics, it should be noted that the city's crime reporting system was modified in March 1966, in a manner that precludes a continuous comparison of crimes (except offenses) across all years. This modification mandated that *all known* incidents be reported and put in their proper category. Before this point in time it was apparently customary for precincts to omit reports for some crimes and to downgrade the seriousness of others.[6] In addition to this empirical discrepancy, the basic data source document, the NYPD *Annual Report*, was not published after 1970. Major crime statistics post-1970 are taken from *Statistical Report: Complaints and Arrests*. This document, which had been published concurrently with the *Annual Report*, unfortunately only contains information regarding major crime categories. Therefore, scrutiny of police activities in supportive services and specialized units must terminate at 1970. All these factors place limitations on the continuity and time span of some of our activity measures.

Activity and Performance[e]

The preceding discussion gives an indication of the variety of functions performed by NYPD. The magnitude of police activities is equally noteworthy.

[e]Detailed data by year and borough are contained in Appendix A, Tables A-1 to A-23.

In 1973 there were over 1 million felonies, misdemeanors, and violations (which include all major crimes) recorded and investigated in New York City. Arrests and summonses for felonies and misdemeanors totaled 220,420 while those for offenses, violations, and traffic infractions as well as those related to other governmental authorities exceeded 3 million in 1970. In the eight years between 1966 and 1973, the investigation of felonies rose by 38 percent, misdemeanors by 9 percent, and violations by 175 percent. Changes in primary and supportive activities within NYPD from 1960 to 1970 (or 1973 as available) are shown in Table 3-1.[f]

The crime statistics are divided into three major categories: (1) felonies, which include the most serious crimes such as murder, rape, assault, robbery, burglary, major narcotics violations, and larceny; (2) misdemeanors, including lesser degrees of some felonies, prostitution, liquor law offenses, etc.; and (3) offenses,[g] which includes lesser degrees of some felonies and misdemeanors, and crimes such as disorderly conduct, unlicensed peddling, loitering, and violations of the city's administrative code, such as unnecessary noise, uncovered rifles, and street obstructions at building sites. In the context of analyzing police activities, we assume that all crimes are investigated. This *does not*, however, imply that all investigations are equal. Investigation can run full gamut from merely recording information of a criminal occurrence when no evidence is available, to extensive search of the scene of a crime, to stake-out and surveillance activity, to interrogation of witnesses and other information gathering, to a combination of all these activities. In some instances no investigation is necessary, as the criminal is caught in the act. While this may happen by chance, it is undoubtedly a more frequent occurrence than might be expected, as many minor crimes are "solved" just by issuing a summons to the offender when a crime is actually observed. Also, criminals are often caught in the act by police officers serving as decoys. This may happen with respect to crimes such as prostitution and narcotics sales, as well as more violent incidents such as a mugging, robbery, or assault. In those cases where the criminal is unknown, it is reasonable to assume that more time and effort is expended on investigation of serious crimes (murder) than on minor ones (larceny). Unfortunately, available crime statistics do not permit us to infer anything about the amount or intensity of police investigatory activity associated with each type of crime.

Considering the crimes included, it is apparent that the largest growth occurred in the least serious types, that is, violations, which rose by 175 percent between 1966 and 1973, after having increased only 12 percent over the previous five years. Much of this growth took place after 1970 but by 1973 violations had *fallen* some 47,000 over the previous year. In terms of police effort, offenses are undoubtedly the least difficult to investigate. Their nature is such that most are discovered and solved simultaneously (such as the previously

---

[f]As mentioned earlier, dual base years, 1960 and 1966, are used for crime investigation statistics due to the shift in reporting procedures.

[g]The "violations" category was referred to as "offenses" in the NYPD *Annual Report* prior to 1967.

given example of the unlicensed peddler) and they are of much less social concern than felonies.

Turning attention to the more serious crimes, we find that felonies had the next largest increase between 1966 and 1973. Felonies are undoubtedly of major importance in terms of investigation because of the seriousness of the crimes involved. They include crimes the average citizen is generally most anxious about—those involving his personal safety and that of his property, murder, rape, assault, robbery, and burglary. Other felonies include grand larceny, automobile theft, and major narcotics violations. These are discussed separately. While total felonies grew by 38 percent between 1966 and 1973, some of the more serious ones showed much more pronounced change. Indeed, murder and nonnegligent manslaughter jumped 130 percent, rape 71 percent, and robbery 209 percent. Although these proportionate increases are major and the nature of the crimes necessitates considerable investigation, it should be pointed out that they represent rather small proportions of total felonies. Murder and rape each constitute *less than* 1 percent of the total, while robbery accounted for 18 percent in 1973. Assault also is a small portion (6%) and did not rise by very much during the period examined. Burglary made up another 36 percent of felonies but increased by only 25 percent. Investigation for all felonies peaked in 1971 and each of the separate felonies shown (except rape) peaked prior to 1973. It appears that investigation of serious crimes has declined somewhat over the later years of the study period.[h] The final crime category, misdemeanors, increased just 9 percent between 1966 and 1973, although it had risen 37 percent in the prior period. However, there were over 110,000 more misdemeanors in the peak year 1970 than in 1973, when there were about 396,000; this represents an enormous decline in just three years.

The second major crime-related activity is arrests and summonses. NYPD activity in this area increased the most for felonies between 1966 and 1973. Arrests for all felonies totaled 91,043 in 1973, 57 percent more than in 1966. Peak activity occurred in 1971, however, with over 11,100 more arrests than in 1973. Relative to investigation, felony arrests increased proportionately more. Arrests for burglary, for example, rose 81 percent between 1966 and 1973, compared with a 25 percent increase in investigations. For the major felonies, however, arrest activity generally did not grow as much as investigation. The disparity is most pronounced in the rape category, where arrests increased just 18 percent, compared with a 71 percent increase in investigations. The most severe felonies account for a small proportion of all felony arrests, ranging from about 2 percent for murder and nonnegligent manslaughter to 19 percent for

[h]The felony category apparently was most strongly affected by the change in reporting procedures between 1965 and 1966. Ignoring the change, the difference in all felonies for that year alone was 83 percent. The NYPD estimate of the "actual" 1965-66 increase (if the revised system had been in effect earlier) was 7.2 percent. See New York City, Police Department, *Annual Report for 1966* (New York: Printing Section, Police Department, City of New York; undated), p. 29.

Table 3-1
Police Department: Activity Indicators

Indicator	Amount[a] (1965)	Index (1960 = 100)	Amount (1973)	Index (1966 = 100)	Peak Amount	Peak Year
Primary Activities						
Crime investigation:						
All felonies	166,075	153	419,477	138	510,048	1971
Murder and nonnegligent manslaughter	684	157	1,680	230	1,891	1972
Rape	1,574	121	3,735	171	3,735	1973
Assault	16,325	148	24,469	105	25,099	1967
Robbery	8,904	135	72,750	309	88,994	1971
Burglary	50,106	142	149,311	125	181,694	1970
Misdemeanors	312,171	137	395,917	109	506,181	1970
Violations	83,996	112	196,824	275	243,854	1972
Arrests and Summonses:						
All Felonies	54,868	154	91,043	157	102,143	1971
Murder and nonnegligent manslaughter	701	164	1,420	203	1,420	1973
Rape	1,352	120	1,721	118	1,721	1973
Assault	12,461	139	13,758	105	13,758	1973
Robbery	5,367	143	17,450	288	19,227	1972
Burglary	8,913	140	16,647	181	16,647	1973
Misdemeanors	139,790	140	129,377	98	259,654	1970
Violations, traffic infractions, and arrest and summonses for other authorities	2,897,282	130	3,187,227[b]	104	3,187,227	1970
Emergency services:	—	—	48,992[c]	176[d]	48,992	1970
Traffic safety— personal injury vehicle accidents:	—	—	48,254[c]	129[d]	49,519	1968

Table 3-1 (cont.)

Indicator	Amount (1970)	Index (1960 = 100)	Peak Amount	Peak Year
Primary Activities—Specialized Units				
Bomb section cases-total:	10,304	1,035	10,304	1970
Harbor precinct:				
Searches	580	652	634	1969
Rescues (where life endangered)	106	342	106	1970
Cooperation with other departments or authorities and special assignments	307	153	573	1965
Accidents, collisions, fires, etc.	89	193	103	1968
Aviation unit:				
Aerial traffic surveys	383	133	1,045	1966
Searches for missing persons, etc.	247	281	466	1968
Escorts, salutes, etc.	456	404	1,404	1967
Missing persons unit:				
Persons reported missing	13,707	144	14,024	1969
Unidentified dead and sick and lost and abandoned children	10,117	50	21,583	1966
Searches for persons missing from other localities	5,580	244	5,580	1970
Supportive Activities				
Police laboratory—criminal investigations assisted by:	50,931	484	50,931	1970
Fingerprint identification—fingerprints processed:	313,570	118	320,280	1969

Ballistics section—cases investigated:	9,354	279	9,354	1970
Photographic section:				
Assignments	5,881	167	6,308	1967
Prisoners photographed	136,383	287	136,383	1970
Licensing:[e]				
Licenses processed, hearings and investigations	136,211	123	139,430	1969
Property clerk:				
Lots of lost, stolen, abandoned, and decedent's property received[f]	884,596	1,519	884,596	1970
Autos received on tow-away program	110,804	473[g]	110,804	1970
Medical unit:				
Examination of recruits and for retirement on physical disability	6,416	213	9,478	1969
Number of x-rays taken	37,500	185[h]	37,500	1970

[a]Net crimes are used as opposed to reported crimes, as the latter figure may include duplicate or erroneous reports of crime.

[b]This figure is for 1970.

[c]The amounts shown for emergency service and traffic safety are for 1970.

[d]The index base is 1960 = 100.

[e]Licenses included here are for firearms, sound devices, taxicabs, and tow trucks and their drivers.

[f]A lot may mean anything from a single article to a truck load of merchandise.

[g]The tow-away program began in 1966, so in this instance 1966 = 100.

[h]The first available listing for x-rays is 1965; therefore, 1965 = 100.

Sources: Derived from New York City, Police Department, *Annual Report*, 1960-1970 (New York: Printing Section, Police Department, City of New York, undated); and New York City, Police Department, *Statistical Report: Complaints and Arrests*, 1971-73 (New York: Office of Programs and Policies, Crime Analysis Section, Police Department, City of New York, December issues).

robbery. Contrary to the peak for investigation of these crimes, arrest activity for individual major crimes peaked in 1973 in *all but one* instance (robbery peaked in 1972). Total arrests for felonies, however, peaked in 1971, as did total investigations.

With respect to the arrest and summons activity for lesser crimes, misdemeanors actually showed a slight drop (2%) between 1966 and 1973, although arrest activity in this area had risen by 40 percent during the period 1960-66. Arrests for other minor crimes (offenses, violations, and traffic infractions), as well as arrests and summons issued at the request of other governmental authorities, are lumped into one category; they went up just slightly over 1966-70. This group includes the majority of all arrest and summons activity, numbering well over 3 million in 1970. By way of a comparison, felonies and misdemeanors combined reached just over 220,000 in 1973.

There are two remaining nonspecialized, primary activities: emergency service and traffic related endeavors. In this latter category, data exist on vehicular accidents involving personal injury. There has been a moderate gain (29%) in activity involving personal injury accidents between 1960 and 1970 with nearly 50,000 incidents handled at the peak.

Emergency services embrace a wide variety of activity, including: releasing trapped people or animals; alleviating dangerous physical conditions (e.g., fallen electrical wires or trees); rendering first aid; and evacuation and assistance at scenes of accidents. In addition, NYPD responds to emergencies at the request of other departments, such as diverting traffic and controlling crowds at fires, or removing sick or injured persons. Emergency responses have shown considerable growth over the decade 1960-70 (76%), peaking in 1970 at 48,992 cases.

As mentioned before, there are several primary activities within NYPD that tend to be performed by specialized personnel units, as opposed to those discussed above, which fall within the purview of routine police duty. Of the specialized units considered here, operations of the Bomb Squad have increased more than any other single unit. Incidents handled by this squad skyrocketed from less than 1,000 in 1960 to 10,304 in 1970.

Activities within other specialized units are considerably more diverse, and therefore, listed separately in Table 3-1 to show the nature of trends. The Harbor Precinct is responsible for general police functions on various bodies of water around New York City; this includes patrol as well as enforcement of state and local regulations regarding navigation. Of the activities enumerated, the greatest change took place in the areas of searches (e.g., for overdue boats, reported submersions, missing persons, and lost property) up 552 percent and rescues of people in distress where life was endangered up 242 percent.

The Aviation Unit also has diverse duties ranging from aerial searches and surveys, escorts, and investigation of complaints to problems involving aircraft. Greatest growth in activity for this unit occurred in its function of performing escorts, salutes, and fire patrols. These rose 304 percent between 1960 and

1970. It should be noted that some of the activities in 1970 were substantially lower than in prior peak years. Escorts, salutes, etc., numbered 456 in 1970 while there were 1,404 such missions in 1967. Similarly, there were 383 aerial traffic surveys in 1970 compared with 1,045 in 1966. While the difference is less pronounced, there were slightly more than half as many searches in 1970 as at peak in 1968. Thus, it appears that many of the major activities of this unit were in a state of decline during the later few years reported on here.

The Missing Persons Unit has responsibility for locating persons reported missing and identifying unidentified sick and dead persons and lost or abandoned children. Activities here have not risen as much as those in other specialized units discussed. While the number of persons reported missing had risen 44 percent by 1970 and persons reported missing from other localities by 144 percent, unidentified dead, sick, and lost children fell to 50 percent of its 1960 level. These all still number in the thousands, however.

The second major grouping of NYPD activities reflects supportive functions. *Supportive activities* are those that assist the police in performance of their primary duties and generally require specialized personnel. Those under consideration here are intimately linked with the investigative function. Thus, we would expect trends in supportive help roughly to parallel trends in investigation of major crimes. In fact, some of the supportive activities considerably outstrip growth in investigations (unfortunately, complete comparison cannot be made as data on supportive activity terminate at 1970).

The number of criminal investigations assisted by the police laboratory went up 384 percent between 1960 and 1970. Laboratory activities expanded more than any other single supportive function under study, with 50,931 laboratory tests performed in 1970. A great deal of the laboratory work involves testing of suspected narcotics. In fact, narcotics comprised 93 percent of all laboratory procedures in 1970 (compared with 63% in 1960). Thus, most of the growth in this activity is related to growth of a particular type of crime. Cases investigated by the Ballistics Section are also of a technical nature and are related to crimes involving firearms. Activity in this section rose 179 percent between 1960 and 1970.

The NYPD Photographic Section's duties range from photographing prisoners and the scene of various criminal occurrences to special assignments such as taking pictures at labor disputes or picketing. Assignments in these latter areas expanded 67 percent over the period under study, while photographing prisoners increased considerably more—187 percent. The last supportive activity considered is fingerprinting. While this increased relatively little, only 18 percent, the volume of activity is high, exceeding 300,000 fingerprints in 1970. This relatively slight increase may be attributable to the removal of some noncriminal fingerprinting responsibilities from NYPD.

The police department also performs a variety of functions that are less easily classified than those discussed thus far. Among these is the issuance of various licenses, including but not limited to, those for use or sale of firearms, taxicabs, tow trucks and their drivers, and sound devices. In addition to issuing licenses, hearings may be held on disapproved applications and suspensions, particularly with respect to taxicab and tow truck drivers. Expansion of licensing activity was moderate between 1960 and 1970, a 23 percent increase, but the volume runs at 136,000-plus per year.

The Office of the Property Clerk is another activity that is difficult to categorize. The function of this office is to receive, record, and dispose of lost, stolen, abandoned, or decedents' property that comes into the possession of NYPD. Greater activity for this office is shown by the increase in "lots" of property received, (a *lot* of property may mean a single item or a collection of items). The growth in property handled has been massive—1,419 percent. More than 884,000 lots were received in 1970 in addition to 110,804 automobiles. Thus, NYPD is involved in the handling processing, and storing of *at least* 1 million pieces of recovered stolen property each year.

The final unit in this group is the Medical Unit, which performs a variety of basic physical examinations as well as administers some treatment. General examinations of both recruits and officers seeking retirement due to physical disability went up over 100 percent since 1960, reaching some 6,400 cases and 37,000 x-rays in 1970. However, examinations were nearly 50 percent higher in the peak year of 1969 at 9,478.

While it is difficult to generalize about the diverse activities presented here, it is clear that virtually all of them have increased and most have increased significantly. With respect to crime-related activities, criminal investigation rose the most (from 1966 to 1970) in the less serious crimes, while arrests and summonses increased most in the more serious crimes. Various other primary activities also outdistanced crime-related primary activities, but it is difficult to be unequivocal about how much is due to the shift in reporting criteria in 1966. On the whole, however, it can safely be stated that the trend in NYPD operations is clearly one of considerable expansion.

The more complex issue of performance measurement (using the term somewhat interchangeably with effectiveness) remains to be dealt with. In effect, this is a replacement or proxy for productivity, a more commonly employed concept. In its more common usage, *productivity* implies division of an output measure by an input measure (in manufacturing, this might be televisions produced per man-hour). However, in almost all public services we lack true measures of output, making productivity analysis difficult, *at best*. Therefore, the related concepts of performance or effectiveness are employed, implying production of an end result, or accomplishment of an objective. The basic concern here is with the end result of police activities.

Using available data from NYPD, there are several measures possible to approximate the concept performance. Since only crime-related data are available as concerns end results, case-clearance rates (proportion of cases cleared) in each major crime category serves as a basic measure of performance. *Clearance* moves a case from an "unsolved" to a "solved" status without regard to court action. This generally occurs by arrest or summons, although in some instances crimes may be attributed to a person unavailable for arrest (due to death, imprisonment, etc.). In addition, several crimes may be attributed to one suspect, allowing multiple clearance from a single arrest. The other performance measure used is the recovery rate for stolen property. Indicators for both measures are shown in Table 3-2.

Crime-clearance rates can be thought of as indicative of how well the police are performing their investigative function. A 100 percent clearance rate means that all *known* crimes have been investigated and solved. For 1973 the highest clearance rate for a large crime category was 63.8 percent for misdemeanors and violations combined. In the more serious crime grouping (felonies), overall

Table 3-2
Police Department: Performance Indicators

Indicator	Rate (1965)	Index (1960 = 100)	Rate (1973)	Index (1966 = 100)	Peak (Post-1966) Rate	Peak (Post-1966) Year
Clearance rates:[a]						
All felonies	34.5	100	19.3	108	24.4	1969
Murder and nonnegligent manslaughter	83.2	93	69.4	92	77.5	1967
Rape	72.7	94	36.9	69	53.5	1966
Assault	65.9	94	50.2	110	50.2	1973
Robbery	42.9	102	18.9	107	27.5	1969
Burglary	28.9	102	14.2	126	20.2	1969
Misdemeanors	49.3	99	42.4	104	49.7	1970
Violations	99.4	100	94.1	95	99.2	1966
				Index (1960 = 100)	Peak (1960-73)	
Property recovery rates:[b]						
Motor vehicles			32.0	35	90.4	1960
Other property			5.0	100	8.1	1969

[a]Percentage of all *known* crimes that have been "investigated and solved."

[b]Dollar value of property recovered relative to dollar value of all property reported stolen.

Sources: Derived from New York City, Police Department, *Annual Report*, 1960-70 (New York: Printing Section, Police Department City of New York, undated); and New York City, Police Department, *Statistical Report: Complaints and Arrests*, 1971-73 (New York: Office of Programs and Policies, Crime Analysis Section, Police Department, City of New York, December issues).

clearance was a low 19.3 percent. Within the major individual felonies considered, murder and manslaughter showed the highest rate, 69.4 percent, and burglary the lowest, 14.2 percent. Clearance for all serious crimes except murder-manslaughter and rape rose between 1966 and 1973, although generally not by appreciable amounts.

Comparing 1973 clearance rates with those prevailing in 1965, however, shows them to be *lower* in 1973, usually by significant amounts. Thus, the increases shown for 1973 are due to the use of dual base years. In 1966, after the advent of the changed reporting system, clearance rates fell sharply for most serious crimes, probably due to the greater incidence of crimes actually recorded. Examples of the change are: rape fell from 72.7 percent in 1965 to 53.5 percent in 1966; robbery, 42.9 percent to 17.7 percent; burglary 28.9 percent to 11.3 percent. It seems clear that the reporting system prior to 1966 had the effect of inflating the crime-solving capacity of the police department.

Clearance rates in the misdemeanor category rose slightly (4%) between 1966 and 1973 to 42.4 percent, while violations declined somewhat during the same period to 94.1 percent. Neither of these less serious crime categories were much influenced by the revised reporting system. Clearance rates for misdemeanors fell from consistently around 50 percent prior in 1965 to a low of 40.9 percent in 1966. Violation clearance rates were over 94 percent from 1960 to 1967, but fell to about 92 percent in 1969. Thereafter they rose as high as 96.2 percent but did not regain the nearly perfect performance of earlier years.

The other performance proxy derived from NYPD reports is the *recovery rate for stolen property*. This is expressed as a percent of the dollar value of stolen property recovered and is shown separately for motor vehicles and all other property. Recovery rates on motor vehicles fell precipitously in the period 1960 to 1973 from 90.4 percent in 1960 to 32.0 percent in 1973; 1960 represented the peak. Effectiveness in the recovery of other property did not decrease absolutely as much but it has never been even as high as 10 percent. The recovery rate was 4.9 percent in 1960 and 5.0 percent in 1973. Values have remained approximately within this range with the exception of 1969 when it jumped way up to 8.1 percent.

The above variables have been chosen to proxy performance due to their availability. It is not implied that they are fully representative of all "performance" by NYPD. Also, under New York City's productivity program[i] a variety of steps have been taken to increase productivity within the department. Examples of activities undertaken or in process of implementation under this program

---

[i]The concept of requiring productivity increases in contract negotiations with uniformed services began in 1970 and extensions of productivity concepts to other city departments occurred in 1971. City of New York, *Productivity Program* (New York, 1972). Discussion of the programs undertaken and their success can be found in Citizens Budget Commission, *New York City's Productivity Program: The Police Department* (New York, 1973), and Edward K. Hamilton, "Productivity: The New York City Approach," *Public Administration Review*, vol. 32 (November-December 1972), p. 791.

(from 1972 to 1973) include: establishment of anticrime patrol teams (police officers in civilian clothing); rescheduling of manpower to provide more officers during high-crime hours; introduction of tactical patrol programs to concentrate resources in high-crime areas; centralized court processing; civilianization of clerical and administrative activities (to free uniformed personnel for street duty); and establishment of auxiliary police (uniformed civilians on patrol in high-crime areas).

While these all seem important steps toward greater productivity, they are not yet fully reflected in the measures we have dealt with. Increases in arrests or crime clearance could be partially attributed to such productivity efforts, but improvement in crime prevention, undoubtedly a major aim of such programs, remain nonquantifiable. However, the important point to be made is that efforts at increased performance or productivity are being undertaken by NYPD, even though we cannot (yet?) measure their impact.

Conclusions

It is apparent from the foregoing discussion that activities of NYPD have expanded considerably over the years 1960 to 1973. Investigation of crime has increased most for the least serious crimes, but has also gone up considerably for the most serious crimes. Growth in arrests has outdistanced investigations in the area of felonies (the only category for which data permit such a comparison). Arrests for lesser crimes have shown little change (a slight decrease for misdemeanors, and a slight increase for other crimes) between 1966 and 1970. The 1973 statistics indicate that investigative activities and, therefore, crimes reported were below their peak levels in most crime categories.

Noncrime and specialized primary activities increased, for the most part, considerably more than crime-related activities. Supportive activities also tended to exhibit the same growth pattern relative to crime-linked activities.

The problem of measuring performance has been discussed. The two measures employed here show slight gains in some cases but, for the most part, decreases. While clearance rates have risen somewhat for major crimes between 1966 and 1973, they remain below the 1965 rate for all felonies and for major felony types. However, it has been noted that pre-1966 clearance rates were overstated due to an underreporting of some crimes; therefore, the validity of comparison between the two periods is lessened.

One other performance measure, recovery rate of stolen property, offers a dismal picture. While the recovery rate for automobiles was high in 1960 (90.4%), it had dropped to about 32 percent by 1970. The recovery rate for other stolen property declined less spectacularly but remained at an extremely low level throughout.

Considering the divergent types of indicators being used, it is inappropriate to make sweeping generalizations concerning performance-effectiveness. It is evident that growth in activity levels, as a rule, far exceeded that of performance. It seems reasonable, therefore, to draw the conclusion that pressure on various NYPD activities swamped the department's capacity to keep performance in pace with activity. During the 1960-73 period, the uniformed force increased only about 27 percent, and this includes an unknown proportion of personnel assigned to "desk jobs" rather than more overt crime-combatant or crime-solving tasks. It seems that since NYPD did not expand its forces to keep pace with rising demands or find other methods of expanding capacity, it was overwhelmed by the growing need for its services and, therefore, suffered a decline in performance. While this is best stated as an assumption, particularly because of the limited availability of data on which to construct indicators, it is consistent with the information available.

Notes

1. City of New York, *Expense Budget for 1971-72* (New York: undated), p. 87.

2. Peter W. Greenwood, *An Analysis of the Apprehension Activities of the New York City Police Department* (New York: New York City RAND Institute, 1970), p. 8. See also the numerous other New York City RAND Studies.

3. Unless otherwise noted, statistics reported herein are taken or derived from New York City, Police Department, *Annual Report* from 1960 to 1970 (New York: Printing Section, Police Department of the City of New York, undated), and/or New York City Police Department, *Statistical Report: Complaints and Arrests* from 1971 to 1973 (New York: Office of Programs and Policies, Crime Analysis Section, Police Department of the City of New York, December issues).

4. *New York Times*, November 12, 1974.

5. Albert J. Reiss, Jr., *Studies in Crime and Law Enforcement in Major Metropolitan Areas*, vol. I (University of Michigan, undated), p. 9.

6. *New York Times*, April 5, 1966.

4 Fire Department

Overview

The Fire Department of New York (FDNY) is charged with the functions of extinguishing fires, protecting life and property in the event of fire and disaster, maintaining and extending the fire alarm system, preventing fires by inspection of buildings and their contents for fire hazards and public education, investigating and determining the cause of fires and enforcing fire-related provisions of the city's Administration Code.[1] While there is a variety of activities performed to fulfill these responsibilities (some of which are conceptually and operationally similar to those of the Police Department), the emphasis within the Fire Department is clearly on fire extinguishment and associated operations.

The 13,558 uniformed employees working for the department in 1972 found their occupation a hazardous one. In this year alone there were 5,849 cases of service-connected injury (uniformed and civilian personnel) including 14 line-of-duty deaths.[2] The growth of injuries (266%) and deaths (100%) between 1961 and 1972 far exceeded that of manpower, which rose by only 17 percent, and points out that fire fighting and associated tasks have become much more hazardous over the years. Employee workloads have also far exceeded manpower growth; 274,785 initial alarms were responded to in 1972, almost 200 percent greater than 1960. More than 5.2 million miles were traveled in performance of duty in 1972 as contrasted to something less than 3 million in 1960.

As is the case with other city departments, there is a wide range of activities within the FDNY.[a] Those that can be considered of a primary nature are fire extinguishment and response to emergency situations, which may range from the evacuation of entire buildings or subways, to the rendering of minor emergency first aid. The Fire Department also has a Marine Unit, with a fleet of 11 fireboats (as of 1969), which is responsible for waterfront and boat fire extinguishment and marine rescues.

Supportive tasks of FDNY includes those intended to prevent fires, such as public education (generally fulfilled by lectures, television broadcasts, and distribution of materials), inspection of building, and the issuance of permits. FDNY also investigates suspicious fires and may actually arrest persons suspected of arson. Other supportive functions include training new recruits, familiarizing employees with new procedures or equipment, and training people

---

[a]Perusal of an *Annual Report* or *Annual Statistics* volume for FDNY will make this diversity in service provision more evident.

other than departmental personnel, including members of other city departments.

Due to the variety and essential nature of vehicles and apparatus, maintenance of equipment is crucial. There were over 520 pumpers or ladder trucks
in operation in 1972 as well as 340 other pieces of equipment. A total of 16,632
repair jobs were performed on this equipment in 1972 in addition to numerous
tests of new apparatus, vehicles, and hoses. FDNY Mask Service Unit inspects
and repairs oxygen masks and related equipment and delivers oxygen cylinders
to fire locations or field depots. Marine equipment requires maintenance, often
involving the use of scuba diving for underwater repairs. The department also has
a research and development unit to test and evaluate new equipment and
technological advances in fire fighting.

FDNY has a photographic unit and a community and news service division.
Along with public relations functions, the latter is charged with assisting in the
provision of emergency housing and helped to locate housing for 5,443 persons
in 1972. The department also maintains a museum, which recorded some 63,000
visitors and 672 guided tours in 1972 and a library, which had nearly 2,000
visitors in 1972.

As is true of any city department or private enterprise, there are general
supportive services such as clerical, administrative, and maintenance functions
for which we have no data. The department has its own medical division, which
examines new personnel as well as sick or injured FDNY employees. This unit
responds to some emergency calls at the scene of fires or emergencies.

Similar to the case of the Police Department (and other government services),
available data can only serve as indicators of activities and performance. No
single measure can be appropriate due to the diversity of departmental
operations. Measures of activity, in terms of answering alarms, fires fought, and
responses to emergencies, represent the most readily available data. Proxy
measures for preventive functions are inspections made and permits issued. None
of the available statistics clearly served the function of a performance indicator;
the concept of performance in fire fighting is discussed after evaluating changes
in activity indicators. Data are available on most indicators from 1960 to 1972.

Activity and Performance[b]

The one activity most clearly associated with any fire department is, of course,
fire extinguishment, measured here by the number of responses to fires (see
Table 4-1). Actually, this is a slight overstatement, as a small percentage of fires
are put out before the arrival of any fire equipment. Even in these cases,
however, it must be ascertained that the fire is completely extinguished and not
likely to spread. This necessitates a certain amount of involvement.

[b]Detailed data by year and borough are contained in Appendix A, Tables A-24 to A-33.

Table 4-1
Fire Department: Activity Indicators

Indicator	Amount (1972)	Index (1960 = 100)	Peak Amount	Peak Year
Primary Activities				
Fires extinguished:				
Total	118,297	194	127,826	1968
Residential	38,218	206	38,218	1972
Commercial	7,394	134	7,394	1972
Public places	2,133	272	2,133	1972
Vacant buildings[a]	6,318	231	7,024	1970
Miscellaneous	70,552	212	81,215	1968
Multiple-alarm fires	516	180	626	1968
False alarms	106,878	655	106,878	1972
Response to emergencies	49,610	294	49,610	1972
Supportive Activities				
Fire prevention activities:				
Buildings inspected	658,719	76	1,600,407	1964
Violation orders and summonses issued	83,561	47	600,802	1964
Permits issued	205,952	80	321,302	1965
School lectures	391	7[b]	18,908	1962
General lectures	313	33[b]	1,705	1968
Investigative activities:				
Number of investigations	8,792	32[b]	47,746	1970
Number of arrests	486	261[b]	624	1969
Medical division:				
Personnel examinations	1,192	22	5,323	1960
Member visits	38,423	240	38,423	1972
Doctors responding to fires	2,649	413	2,649	1972

[a]Fires in vacant buildings are also counted in the appropriate structural category in 1972 only. Therefore, the subcategories exceed the total by 6,318.

[b]1961 = 100.

Sources: Fire Department, City of New York, *Annual Report*, 1960-69; and *Annual Statistics*, 1970-72.

There were 118,297 fires in 1972, 94 percent more than in 1960. Large as this volume is, it falls almost 10,000 short of 1968, the peak year of those under study. The 1968 figure represented a drastic upward shift in just *one* year (almost 40% over 1967), while the number of fires since then has gradually receded to the 1972 level.

Within subcategories by type of fire, miscellaneous fires accounted for the largest number in 1972 (60%). This category includes rubbish fires; brush fires; bonfires; fires in transit or railroad yards; ship and vessel fires; transportation fires; fires in motor vehicles and abandoned or derelicit vehicles; fires in manholes, tunnels, or bridges; and miscellaneous other fires. Of the latter, rubbish fires accounted for the largest portion in 1972 (58%), motor vehicle and abandoned motor vehicles another 25 percent, and brush fires 11 percent. A few other categories each accounted for more than 1 percent of all miscellaneous. While this type represents the largest number of fires, in general, they are among the more easy to extinguish.

Residential fires comprise the second largest category numbering in excess of 38,000 in 1972.[c] These fires are more difficult to deal with because of the potential danger to lives of residents and the greater possibility that firemen will be called on for evacuation, rescue, or first aid.

Residential and miscellaneous fires combined made up 92 percent of all fires in the city in 1972. Those in commercial buildings accounted for another 6 percent and in public places (including airports, hospitals, schools, churches, transit stations, theaters, etc.) 2 percent. The latter category presents serious potential danger to a large number of people and raises the possibility of rapid mass evacuation by the Fire Department. Considering the greater hazards public fires present to the fire department and the public, they fortunately occur rather infrequently. However, it should be noted that fires in public places exhibited the largest growth (172%) over a 12-year period, albeit on the smallest base. The least amount of increase, on the other hand, was in commercial fires (34%).

A final subcategory is fires in vacant buildings. These were enumerated separately prior to 1972, both as a subcategory and as reflected in an appropriate structural category. As a distinct fire category, fires in vacant buildings rose by 13 percent between 1960 and 1972, to 6,318, yet dropped slightly from the peak in 1970.

The Marine Administration Unit is a specialized unit that performs primary activities. Unfortunately, its activities have not been recorded separately in the FDNY *Annual Report*. However, there were 90 fires in ships and vessels listed under the miscellaneous category in 1972 and 160 fires in piers and shipyards; while in 1960 there were 75 ship and vessel fires and 114 in piers and shipyards. These represent increases of 20 percent and 40 percent, respectively. It is most likely that the Marine Unit responded to most, if not all, of these incidents. Given the volume of change in marine fires, it would seem that activities of this specialized unit have not increased by nearly as much as those of the land-based forces of the department.

[c]Fires in all structural categories in 1972 are somewhat overstated compared to previous years due to an inclusion of vacant buildings in the structural category; prior to 1972 fires in vacant buildings were shown separately. Much of the "overstatement" probably occurred in the residential category, which had a particularly large increase (4,724) fires between 1971 and 1972.

In addition to actual fires, FDNY responds to a huge number of false alarms, also considered here as an activity measure. There were 106,878 false alarms in 1972 representing a staggering 555 percent expansion over 1960. This is only 11,419 fewer responses than to *real* fires. While false alarms obviously do not entail the same work or danger as extinguishing fires, they do entail the time, effort, and danger of travel to and from the scene of an alarm. Also, they create the hazard of delayed response to real fires, but by how much is not known. It is sufficient to note that an enormous amount of time and resources is wasted in responding to false alarms; it is also disquieting to note that they now number almost as many as real fires.

Another measure of activity is response to nonfire emergencies. These include general emergencies, such as the need for first aid, water leaks and floods, collapses and cave-ins, as well as incidents where there appears to be an appreciable danger of fire or explosion such as leaks of flammable or explosive substances. Responses to such emergencies numbered 49,610 in 1972, 194 percent more than in 1960.

The final primary tasks considered are the evacuation of people from dangerous situations and the rendering of first aid. Unfortunately, data on these two functions are available only for 1972. However, in that year alone, 35,888 evacuations and 6,423 instances of first aid administration were performed. These include both fire and nonfire incidents.

Although we have considered the quantity of fire and nonfire activity, there has been no consideration thus far of the degree of difficulty or danger involved in extinguishing fires. A simple enumeration tends to treat all incidents equally with respect to size, difficulty, danger, and resource claims. In reality there can be vast differences among fires. Variance along these dimensions are not reflected in the data and remain one of those nonquantifiable facets of fire fighting yet to be dealt with. One statistic that does give some indication of the "difficulty" dimension, however, is the number of multiple alarm fires. A *multiple alarm* represents an instance when the initial response of fire apparatus and personnel is inadequate to cope with the situation without calling in assistance. This indicates the occurrence of an unusually large and/or unusually dangerous fire. In 1972 there were 516 instances of multiple alarms as compared with 287 in 1960. Multiple-alarm fires have become much more prevalent in the later study years, with the greatest number (626) occurring in 1968. At the opposite extreme of the "difficulty continuum" we can consider the number of fires extinguished *before* the arrival of any FDNY equipment. This went from 5,052 in 1960 to 6,781 in 1972 (the figures refer to structural fires only). However, "extinguished fires" accounted for 18 percent of all structural fires in 1960 as opposed to only 14 percent in 1972. Thus, it appears that demands on the Fire Department are increasing along the entire continuum of fire fighting.

Two related concerns falling within the fire-prevention sphere are the inspection of buildings for fire hazards and the issuance of violation orders or summonses when hazardous conditions are uncovered. In 1972 there were 658,719 inspections with 83,561 violation orders and summonses issued. Both these figures are considerably lower than 1960, inspections by 24 percent and violations and summonses by 53 percent. There is an even greater decline from the peak level for both of these activities when there were 1,600,407 inspections and 600,802 violations and summonses issued. It is quite evident from these data that this facet of prevention activity is receiving considerably less attention. Another facet of FDNY's preventive operations is its regulatory function as indicated by number of permits issued. Permits are issued to establishments handling or storing flammable or explosive materials, such as fuel oil, kerosene, acids, gases, paints, or ammunition. The number of permits issued fell 20 percent between 1960 and 1972 to 205,952, while peak activity occurred in 1965 with 321,302 permits issued.

FDNY's other major preventive endeavor falls under the rubric public education. This includes the distribution of fire prevention literature, television and radio announcements, lectures, and door-to-door information campaigns. Unfortunately, statistics on all of these activities were kept in a very spotty manner throughout the study period. Prior to 1966 information dissemination was handled by the Division of Public Information and Education. In 1966 the Community Relations Bureau was established and assumed these duties. The major facet for which data are available from 1961 on are fire prevention lectures delivered at schools, community, civic, fraternal, or similar organizations. The number of lectures in schools has fallen more than 90 percent, from 5,861 in 1961 to 391 in 1972. However, in 1962 18,908 fire prevention lectures were delivered with roughly 15,000 given each following year from 1964 to 1967; they then plummeted to the current level. While this aspect of prevention has followed an erratic pattern, it is clear that school lectures are nearly a thing of the past. General lectures have followed a similar, but not so marked, downward trend (from 950 in 1961 to 313 in 1972) and display a range from 129 in 1965 to 1,705 in 1968. The volume of lectures has risen at certain times in response to specific campaigns. For example, in 1967 in excess of 16,000 lectures (not classified as general lectures) were given in conjunction with a false alarm-prevention campaign.

Data on door-to-door campaigns to disseminate fire-prevention and safety information are available only between 1960 and 1965. The number of households involved averaged about 431,000 per year after 1960 with over 900,000 persons contacted. This activity apparently ceased after 1965 (or simply was not recorded). In 1969, however, a mobile education unit was created, which also spread information to individuals. In its first year of operation 63,603 persons were contacted but by 1972 this had fallen to 22,672.

In addition to educating the general public, the department has also worked closely with specialized groups such as employees of hotels or hospitals. However, the level of these activities has been a fraction of those for the general public. In short, educational efforts related to fire prevention have exhibited wide variation but a general drift downward over the period examined.

It has been mentioned that FDNY has an investigatory function and may arrest people for arson. Prior to 1970 all building fires were investigated by fire marshalls and/or chief officers while after that only suspicious fires or those where the cause was not readily ascertained were investigated. In 1972, 8,792 fires were investigated by fire marshalls as compared with 27,874 in 1961 and 47,746 at the peak in 1970. In 1971, however, with the change in criteria for investigation, there were about 14,900. The second investigation proxy is the number of arrests made for arson or related offenses. In 1972, 486 were made, a 161 percent rise from 1961. The peak year (1969) was considerably higher, however, at 624. Considering the variance in these two indicators of investigative service, it is not obvious whether there has been an overall upward or downward trend in this aspect of FDNY operations. The current level does remain, however, well below past peaks.

The final supportive category examined concerns the Medical Division. This division performs physical examinations for new personnel, promotion and fitness, and pension claims; it examines FDNY members who are ill or injured (including home and hospital visits), and responds to some fires. Actual examination of personnel declined considerably (78%) between 1960 and 1972 to a level of 1,192. On the other hand, member visits to the medical division showed a sharp increase (140%), attaining 38,423 visits by 1972. The number of doctors going to the scene of a fire also rose dramatically (313%) with 2,649 responses in 1972 compared with only about 600 in 1960. On the whole, it can be stated that growth in this division more than offset the decline recorded.

The concept of performance is particularly difficult to define and measure for the Fire Department. Some indicators that appear to be reasonable proxies for performance would be the amount of time spent extinguishing fires, the value of property saved, or the value of property destroyed. The former would clearly have to be standardized by class of fire since it would not be reasonable to compare time spent extinguishing a small brush fire with that of a large structural fire. Unfortunately, data of this nature over a long time period are not kept. Nor can other performance-related indicators be derived from what data do exist.

However, several notable advances have been made under New York's productivity program and they represent the type of nonquantifiable advances in performance not yet reflected in departmental statistics. Two of the major achievements, adaptive response and "rapid water," have occurred as a result of cooperation between the New York City RAND Institute and the Fire Department.[d] The Adaptive Response System (which is in effect at selected locations during certain hours), involves reducing the number of units that respond to alarms from alarm boxes with a history of a high proportion of false alarms. This eliminates some of the wasted effort associated with false alarms

---

[d]A summary of work performed by the New York City RAND Institute in conjunction with the FDNY can be found in Edward H. Blum, *Urban Fire Protection: Studies of the Operations of the New York Fire Department* (New York: New York City RAND Institute, 1971).

and by freeing manpower provides better protection in the event a fire occurs elsewhere while units are responding to a false alarm.[3] "Rapid water" is the result of a chemical process that reduces friction inside hoses, thus providing a more rapid and greater volume of water flow, which helps increase effectiveness in fire extinguishment. It also allows use of lighter hoses, which permits greater mobility and a reduction in manpower per hose.

An additional measure designed to improve performance is also being tested. This is a two-way, voice-communication, street-alarm box, which enables a dispatcher to determine the nature of the emergency being reported and then send an appropriate complement of equipment and manpower. It is anticipated that this system will help reduce false alarms or limit the number of units sent to potential false alarms and better allocate resources in accordance with need.[4] Other increases recorded under New York's productivity program include (in fiscal 1971-72) purchase of 75 new fire vehicles and development of a pilot program that provides fire officers with specific information about hazardous buildings.[5]

Conclusions

All Fire Department primary activities exhibited substantial expansion between 1960 and 1972. Actual fires went up by *less* than false alarms and nonfire emergencies, however. Activities also became more hazardous as indicated by both the increase in multiple-alarm fires and in injuries to department personnel. Supportive activities, in general, showed an opposite trend. For example, all preventive activities declined markedly. Of the few supportive activities that did increase, arrests and some medical division activities were most notable.

It is apparent that large gains in primary activities—94 percent increase in fires; 194 percent increase in emergencies; and a 555 increase in false alarms— were handled with only a modest 17% growth in manpower, implying gains in productivity. At the same time, however, operations within supportive functions such as fire prevention and investigation dropped off, perhaps indicating a trade-off in manpower from the latter to the former.

Notes

1. City of New York, *Expense Budget for 1971-72* (New York: undated), p. 198.

2. Unless otherwise noted, statistical data are taken or derived from Fire Department-City of New York, *Annual Report*, for the years 1960 through 1969; and Fire Department-City of New York, *Annual Statistics*, for 1970 through 1972.

3. Edward K. Hamilton, "Productivity: The New York City Approach," *Public Administration Review*, vol. 32 (November-December 1972), pp. 790-91.

4. Herbert Ranschburg and Nicholas Moy, *The New York City Fire Department: Present Achievements and Present Problems* (New York: Citizens Budget Commission, 1973), pp. 6-11.

5. City of New York, Fire Department Productivity Program, *Productivity Program* (New York: City of New York, 1972), pp. 1-3.

5

Social Services

Overview

The term social services is employed here in the narrow sense of welfare and those related services for the poor that are administered by the Department of Social Services (DSS).[a] DSS has been delegated responsibility for: providing financial, medical, and other assistance to persons in need and assisting them in returning to a self-supporting status; providing shelter for homeless adults and care for neglected and dependent children; and rendering emergency or disaster assistance to the city.[1] These broad mandates are transformed into numerous specific policy outputs, which include the distribution of various forms of income supplements, counseling and job referral, operation of shelter homes for homeless or delinquent children, placement of children for foster care or adoption, operation of shelters for homeless adults, provision of dental and optical care, and determination of eligibility for Medicaid assistance. These duties were performed in 1973 by a staff of 32,575. Personnel attached to DSS has increased sharply; 1973 employment was 27 percent more than in 1970 and 292 percent more than in 1960.[2] Employment in this department has shown growth far in excess of any of the other major service departments under study here, nearly five times the next closest. DSS has expanded from the smallest department in 1960, by several thousand employees, to the second largest next to the Police Department.

Acquiring operational measures of activities falling in the purview of social services is difficult because one must, to a large extent, deal in intangibles. That is, usually we cannot measure directly the type or extent of assistance that is actually provided to those in need. Even more troublesome is just how to determine the impact or efficacy of the help actually rendered. One hour with a counselor could mean a job for one person and a waste of time for another with no appreciable difference between the two persons in terms of resources expended.

The main charge of DSS, in broad terms, are those functions mentioned above. Of prime concern is the distribution of welfare payments and the attendant tasks of determining eligibility, counseling, job referral, etc.—activities

---

[a]Other social service-related activities, such as manpower training, Headstart, community-action programs, community-health centers, drug-addiction clinics, and the like fall under the aegis of New York's Human Resources Administration (HRA) of which the Department of Social Services is one component.

usually performed by caseworkers and/or social workers. Other primary activities include the provision of shelter and personal care for children and adults; adoption and foster home placement of children with continued supervision after placement; operation of dental and optical clinics; and Medicaid administration. Unfortunately, available statistics do not completely define many DSS efforts. For the various welfare services rendered to the poor, the only data available are number of people (or cases) receiving various forms of income assistance. Similarly, we can obtain only a simple count of the number of persons served in the other types of primary care, without knowing the exact nature, extent, or intensity of care rendered.

Supportive activities for DSS are numerous and diverse. The paperwork and record keeping generated in a welfare system as large as New York City's—500,000 public-assistance cases representing 1.3 million people as of 1973—is extensive, as are the routine clerical and administrative tasks.[3] For example, shelter care included as a primary activity gives rise to supportive services such as housekeeping, building and grounds maintenance, kitchen and dining room operation, linen service, and recreation opportunities. Child welfare entails supportive services performed by doctors, nurses, and psychologists in addition to actual physical shelter and feeding.

Two major indicators are used for the primary function of income assistance: These are the number of cases receiving assistance broken down into various aid categories (which are aid to families with dependent children, home relief, old-age assistance, aid to the blind, and aid to the disabled) and the number of applications received for assistance broken down in the same way. These are really proxies for a wide array of services associated with income supplementation. The number of cases indicates, at a minimum, that some regular financial support is being provided. It may also be considered to reflect some (albeit unknown) level of counseling and referral activity and some (again unknown) amount of checking for continued eligibility. Assistance applications, on the other hand, may be considered to indicate investigation to determine eligibility, referral to an appropriate assistance category, substantial amounts of paperwork, and personal interviews with applicants.

Indicators for adult-shelter care are the number of meals provided and the average daily census, while for child welfare we use the number of persons under care. For dental and optical services, procedures performed (of all types) by clinics is the activity indicator. This can, of course, encompass wide variation in the extent of care actually provided.

One difficulty exists due to the manner in which data are collected by DSS. Most statistics are assembled on a monthly basis but these cannot just be summed to obtain a yearly total since this would involve serious double counting of individuals receiving assistance for more than one month—most of the recipients. Fortunately, some data are maintained on an "average monthly" basis. Where these averages are not available, the month of January is used as a proxy for the average level of activity over the year.

Before discussing activity and performance, it should be emphasized that there are numerous exogenous factors that affect the amount of work required of DSS. Federal and state governments both influence the level of welfare activity by establishing basic criteria for eligibility. This affects the number of persons receiving assistance, one basic indicator. For a recent example of just how much federal regulations can influence case loads, in January 1974 people under the old-age-, blind-, and disabled-assistance categories were converted to the Federal Supplemental Security Income program. The number of cases receiving public assistance in New York City fell from 491,261 in December 1973 to 299,281 in January 1974, with this decline almost entirely attributable to the change in federal regulations. In a similar vein, an easing of eligibility requirements would tend to increase DSS applications and caseloads. An example of the state's influence on activity is the enactment of Medicaid legislation by New York State in 1966. This had the effect of adding a completely new set of responsibilities on top of those already performed by DSS, that is determining Medicaid eligibility and then processing and paying claims for service.

Activity and Performance[b]

Looking at the average monthly number of cases receiving assistance in Table 5-1, one is struck by the immense growth in certain categories. Total assistance cases rose 268 percent between 1960 and 1973. Cases under aid to families with dependent children (AFDC) increased 422 percent; aid to the disabled, 348 percent; home relief, 244 percent; and old-age assistance, 71 percent. The category with the smallest growth (14%) was blind assistance but it represents a miniscule proportion of total cases. Greatest growth occurred in the largest category, AFDC, which accounts for about one-half of all welfare cases. All of the major aid categories reached a peak in 1972. One can say unequivocally that DSS activities associated with the under-care population have risen drastically over the 13-year period examined.

Growth trends in public assistance can be further clarified by considering the changing share of total assistance that is accounted for by specific aid categories, shown in Table 5-2. It is evident that the case load has shifted toward AFDC, while old-age assistance has fallen a like amount. These two had similar shares in 1960 (35% of the total in AFDC and 31% in old age) while AFDC accounted for almost one-half of the aid by 1973, with old-age assistance dropping to 14 percent. There have been some additional shifts between 1970 and 1973. In particular, home relief and AFDC both had slight decreases in their share. In addition to the large growth in AFDC, aid to the disabled has increased its share significantly over the latest few years of the study period. This may be due in

bDetailed data by year and borough are contained in Appendix A, Tables A-34 to A-41.

Table 5-1
Department of Social Services: Activity Indicators

Indicator	Amount (1973)	Index (1960 = 100)	Peak Amount	Year
Welfare Activities:				
Average monthly no. of cases				
Total	497,655	368	515,259	1972
Aid to families with dependent children[a]	247,916	522	252,129	1972
Home relief	64,291	344	77,232	1968
Old-age assistance	71,895	171	75,328	1972
Aid to the disabled	110,694	448	110,694	1973
Blind assistance	2,860	114	2,860	1973
Average monthly no. of applications received				
Total	17,567	155	21,286	1971
Aid to families with dependent children[a]	6,674	171	8,189	1970
Home relief	5,810	121	9,460	1968
Old-age assistance	1,262	93	1,873	1971
Aid to the disabled	3,767	303	5,453	1971
Blind assistance	34	77	46	1968
Adult Shelter Care:[b]				
Average daily census	2,153	57	3,838	1961
Meals provided	194,663	62	338,517	1961
Child Welfare:[b]				
Persons under care during the month	47,135[c]	237	47,135	1971
Dental and Optical Care:[b]				
Procedures performed by dental clinics	14,887	48	47,205	1965
Procedures performed by optical clinics	4,813[d]	186	4,813	1967

[a]This includes both AFDC and AFDC-unemployed parent.
[b]As of January of each year.
[c]For January 1971, latest year available.
[d]For January 1967, latest year available.
Source: City of New York, Human Resources Administration, *Monthly Statistical Report*, January 1960 through January 1974 (New York: no date, mimeographed).

part to the fact that drug addicts may be eligible for public assistance under this category.

The second welfare-activity indicator is the average monthly number of applications received. This can be linked to a heightened activity in determining

Table 5-2
Public-assistance Categories as a Percentage of Total Public Assistance

	Percent of Total Aid		
Aid Category	1960	1970	1973
Aid to families with dependent children	35	52	49
Home relief	14	17	14
Old-age assistance	31	16	14
Aid to the disabled	18	14	22
Blind assistance	2	1	1

Source: City of New York, Human Resources Administration, *Monthly Statistical Report*, January 1960 through January 1974 (New York: no date, mimeographed).

eligibility, conducting interviews, processing forms, referral, and counseling. The average number of applications has not risen at a rate anywhere approaching that of the under-care case loads. Total applications rose by 55 percent to 17,567 a month. The only category with an unusually high jump is aid to the disabled, where applications increased 203 percent. Of all the categories, only one showed a major drop in applications: blind assistance fell 23 percent. However, this category is virtually meaningless as compared to others running only some 34 applications per month.

Among the welfare activities of DSS that do not entail income supplements is care for homeless adults in shelters. This activity has shown a marked decline. Average daily census dropped 43 percent, to 2,153 in 1973, while meals provided fell 38 percent, to 194,663. If these figures are taken as representative of a typical month, then approximately 26,000 nights of lodging and over 2 million meals were provided in 1973 alone. While this represents a substantial lessening of adult care, the volume remains far from trivial.

Child-welfare activities present somewhat of a problem in that statistics on the varied services have not been recorded consistently throughout the study period. The only statistic available over a prolonged period is the number of persons under care during a month. As of January 1971 this was 47,135, 137 percent more than January 1960. However, this status does not imply any particular level of activity—care can range from an "active file," which requires no service at all in a given month, to persons who received a wide variety of attention. The intensity and type of care simply cannot be ascertained. Looking at a more recent period (January 1973), we can get a better understanding of the type of work performed to promote child welfare. In that month alone, almost 2,000 applications of various kinds—for children requiring service, reports of child abuse or neglect, preventive service, foster or adoptive parents—were received. Almost 2,500 case studies were performed and 3,600 instances of home counseling provided.

While the extent of child-shelter care provided is less clear the following is the distribution of children remaining under city aegis as of January 1973: shelter, 310; maternity shelter, 168; juvenile detention centers, 156. It seems quite likely that higher levels of service provision may have been given over the year. In juvenile detention centers, for example, turnover was high with 562 people added to the population and 541 removed. Turnover for other forms of care was much lower with only 74 added to the maternity-shelter population and 54 removed and 135 added to general shelters and 170 removed. Although we cannot examine these figures over time, the level of activity does appear significant, especially if we assume that approximately the same level is provided during each month of the year and that turnover is comparable.

The final primary activities under consideration here are the provision of dental and optical care in clinics and the administration of Medicaid. Dental care fell 52 percent from 1960 to 1973, as indicated by dental work performed. In 1973, 14,887 dental procedures[c] were recorded, considerably fewer than the peak of 47,205 attained in 1965. In January 1967, 4,813 optical procedures were performed, an 86 percent rise over 1960. After this year optical care was not made available. It has previously been mentioned that DSS has responsibility for determining eligibility for Medicaid assistance and the processing of payment claims. While statistics on this function are not published, some information is available on general trends. All persons receiving public assistance are eligible for Medicaid, as well as those considered medically indigent. Medicaid enrollees other than public-assistance recipients totaled 201,447 on January 31, 1972, a major decline from December 31, 1969, when there were 415,321 enrollees.[4] The magnitude of these figures gives some indication as to the amount of work entailed in processing applications and determining eligibility. The other major component of Medicaid administration is processing claims for payment. Data are not available for this activity but since there were roughly 1.5 million enrollees in 1972 (including public-assistance recipients) it is evident that claim processing would be a tremendous task even with only one claim per person.

The concept of performance is difficult to apply in the area of social services.[d] True performance would necessarily reflect a removal of need for public assistance due to efforts on the part of DSS in securing employment. It is clear that an elimination of need could also come about *without any* DSS help at all. Similarly, cases can be closed for a wide variety of other reasons unrelated to need, such as failure to comply with regulations, change in status producing ineligibility, death, or moving to another jurisdiction. Cases that have been transferred to other aid categories are also lumped in with cases closed.

Our proxy indicators for performance are the number of cases closed, the

[c]A procedure could range from a simple examination to extremely complex dental or optical work.

[d]See Robert Davis, "Measuring Effectiveness of Municipal Services," *Management Information Service*, ICMA (August 1970), pp. 24-26, for some suggestions.

number closed due to employment, and the number closed due to ineligibility. The latter may be considered a performance proxy because it is one of DSS's responsibilities to ascertain whether recipients remain eligible for assistance. Similarly, DSS encourages employable recipients to seek employment and thus performs some job referral activities. Indicators are all shown in Table 5-3 by assistance category for January of each year under study. Unfortunately, none are available for performance in areas other than financial assistance.[e]

Using the performance indicator case closings, we can say that considerable improvement has occurred between 1960 and 1973. Total cases closed rose 212 percent reaching 21,307 by January 1973. The largest increase occurred in AFDC with a 284 percent increase. Home-relief and aid-to-the-disabled closings

Table 5-3
Department of Social Services: Performance Indicators

Indicator	Amount (1/73)	Index (1/60 = 100)	Peak Amount	Peak Year
Welfare Activities				
Cases closed:				
Total	21,307	312	21,307	1973
Aid to families with dependent children	8,791	384	8,791	1973
Home relief	7,344	324	8,595	1969
Old-age assistance	1,334	140	1,491	1972
Aid to the disabled	3,787	304	5,390	1972
Blind assistance	51	75	68	1960
Cases closed due to employment:				
Total	1,031	66	1,726	1966
Aid to families with dependent children	422	59	1,070	1966
Home relief	519	74	1,108	1968
Old-age assistance	6	16	37	1960
Aid to the disabled	81	74	145	1970
Blind assistance	3	43	7	1960
Cases closed due to ineligibility:				
Total	1,006	274	1,006	1973
Aid to families with dependent children	709	272	709	1973
Aid to the disabled	294	277	294	1973
Blind assistance	3	300	3	1973

Source: City of New York, Human Resources Administration, *Monthly Statistical Report*, January 1960 through January 1974 (New York: no date, mimeographed).

[e]It is not clear what they would be at any rate since performance in these areas remains vague and hard to define.

both also rose by more than 200 percent, while blind-assistance case closings showed the only decrease (but with less than ten cases in all).

Cases closed due to employment have fallen sharply in every category while overall they dropped 34 percent. Only 1,031 cases were closed due to employment in January 1973, which represents a mere 5 percent of all cases closed. Only two categories, AFDC and home relief, showed a number of cases closed due to employment that could be considered of any consequence. But once again, the number is small with respect to the overall scope of the welfare population. Similarly, cases closed due to ineligibility numbered very few, just 1,006 in 1973. However, this 1973 level of closures for ineligibility in all categories recorded was considerably greater than found in earlier periods.

In considering performance as measured by case closure due to employment one should exert caution in interpretation. We cannot simply assume that employment was secured through DSS efforts, although this does occur. On the other hand, even if we assume DSS tried and failed to help welfare recipients secure employment, we cannot regard this as just poor performance on the part of DSS. Factors determining unemployment in our society are too numerous, complex, and interrelated and large numbers of people depend on and receive public assistance because they are virtually unemployable for any of a number of reasons. General economic conditions also have a profound effect on DSS "success" by defining the economic milieu in which employment is sought, the same is true of performance as measured by number of cases closed due to employment.[f]

Under New York City's productivity program, DSS efforts have focused on management functions, more precise determination of client eligibility, and a reduction of fraud. Concerning the latter two areas, a face-to-face recertification program has been implemented, whereby the head of a household is required to appear for an interview to establish continued eligibility. Between the months of March and October of 1973, these efforts resulted in a closing of 17 percent of the cases processed under this program. Most of these closings were due to a failure to report for the interview. This may mean that some of these clients were eligible for assistance, subsequently reapplied, and were again placed on the welfare rolls.

Other productivity efforts include computerization of records to enable more efficient management and control over welfare operation and payments and more accurate information on caseloads. A centralized, automated case-closing system was installed, reducing the number of time-consuming forms to be filled out and the time lag between client notification of case closure and cessation of checks. In addition, a management-reporting system has been implemented whereby auditors regularly check various income-maintenance centers along

[f]Unemployment rates among certain population groups often reach 30-40 percent or more. New York's high concentration in these categories makes welfare roles especially responsive to overall economic conditions.

several dimensions, including error rates. In this way localized problems within specific centers can be identified and dealt with more effectively.

Performance in the productivity sense has also been increased in the area of clerical operations performed by the income-maintenance specialists who deal with establishment of eligibility and determination of appropriate public-assistance category and level of support. Output for these workers has gone up from 8.6 transactions per man-day in July 1972 to 9.6 as of August 1973.[5]

Conclusions

There can be little doubt that the growth of public-assistance activities in DSS has been significant. At least part of this can be traced to an increased federal interest in reducing poverty during the mid-1960s. Various War on Poverty programs increased knowledge of available forms of assistance among the poor, broke down reluctance to ask for help, and reduced the stigma attached to "being on welfare." Receipt of income assistance has come to be increasingly thought of as a right, by both the poor and the nonpoor. These factors have undoubtedly played a major role in swelling assistance case loads in New York City.[g]

In the area of social services, more than in many other public endeavors, statistics can be deceptive. The number of people receiving welfare checks, while certainly important in itself, may be less significant than quantity and quality of counseling or similar services, both personal and employment oriented. This is the epitome of the nonmeasurable "output," which frustrates research efforts. There is clearly a need to find ways of accounting for these intangibles in order to deal more completely and meaningfully with the concept of municipal performance and output. For the moment, suffice it to say that public assistance activity has risen markedly, strongly suggesting that the attendent intangible outputs have likewise grown.

Regarding performance, there is a serious problem of definition and measurement. In terms of overall case closings and those due to ineligibility, performance has improved. In terms of closings due to the actual employment of welfare recipients, which is a much more appealing indicator, there has been a *drop* in performance. However, it has been noted that the degree to which these variables do represent DSS performance is likely to be modest; better data are clearly needed in order to examine performance in a realistic manner useful as an input to public-sector evaluation.

Notes

1. City of New York, *Expense Budget for 1971-72* (New York: undated), p. 220.

---

[g]Andrew Hacker speaks of this in his book *The New Yorkers* (New York: Mason/Charter, 1975), esp. chap. 4.

2. Employment data were taken from the City of New York, Department of Personnel, Civil Service Commission, *Annual Report* (New York: 1959 and 1969); and City of New York, *Schedule Supporting the Executive Budget for 1974-75* (New York: no date).

3. Unless otherwise indicated, statistics are taken or derived from City of New York, Human Resources Administration, *Monthly Statistical Report*, January 1960 through January 1974 (New York: no date, mimeographed). See also Charles Brecher, *Where Have All the Dollars Gone?* (New York: Praeger Publishers, 1974), for background detail.

4. City of New York, Department of Health, *Materia Medicaid: New York City—A Compendium of Selected Data on Trends in Medicaid 1966-71* (New York: August 1972).

5. Herbert Ranschburg and James R. Janz, *New York City's Productivity Program: The Human Resources Administration, The Administration of Welfare* (New York: Citizens Budget Commission, 1975), pp. 15-32.

6

Health and Hospital

Overview

The "health and hospital" designation is somewhat misleading in that hospital functions are the primary focus of this study. Hospital care is provided by three types of facilities in New York City:[a] municipal hospitals (under the Health and Hospital Corporation), which provide care regardless of ability to pay; voluntary hospitals (often affiliated with religious or other organizations), which serve both paying and nonpaying patients; and proprietary hospitals, which are profit-making entities serving private physicians and their patients. The Health and Hospital Corporation (HHC) was established as a "super agency" in 1970 to maintain and operate the city's hospital system.[b]

In addition to this major administrative reorganization, another change occurred during the study period that had an impact on trends in hospital service; this was the enactment of federal Medicare legislation and New York State's Medicaid program in 1966. A major outcome of these programs was an enablement of those in need of health care to make a choice between public and private medical care even if their own financial resources would not enable them to pay for private care. It appears that enactment of these programs resulted in a slight shift in hospital use in favor of private rather than public facilities and, in addition, may have encouraged more widespread use of all medical facilities.

The corporate hospital system is operated with the general aim of providing hospital care for those individuals who do not have the financial resources to obtain private care. HHC has responsibility over nineteen hospitals with in excess of 10,000 beds, situated in every borough of New York, as follows: eight in Manhattan, four each in the Bronx and Brooklyn, two in Queens, and one in Staten Island.

Medical services offered by HHC, like those of every other city department, are myriad. Hospital services can be categorized by type of patient care, such as general inpatient, ambulatory (i.e., emergency room and outpatient), long term, psychiatric, tubercular, and drug addiction. These broad categories do not delineate the specific, individual treatment that patients receive (which would

---

[a]Corporate and HHC will be used interchangeably to refer to New York City municipal hospitals both before and after the formation of HHC.

[b]Other health-related services such as community-health centers, communicable-disease activities, maternal- and child-health services, institutional inspection, laboratory services, and vital statistics fall under the aegis of the New York Health Services Administration. See City of New York, *Expense Budget for 1971-1972* (New York: undated), p. 394.

include attention such as physical examinations, operations performed, babies delivered, bones set, laboratory tests, x-rays, drugs administered, therapy, and other specialized care) but they can be considered as a primary dimension of the corporate system's medical activity.[c]

The complexity of hospital operations and the plethora of nonmedical attention required by patients necessitate a great many supportive functions. Many of these entail direct personal, but nonmedical, care of patients. Such supportive services include food, linen, pharmacy operations, distribution of medical and nonmedical equipment and supplies, maintenance, elevator operations, ambulance, medical records, and miscellaneous other clerical and administrative tasks. Analysis of each of these leads one rapidly into an empirical quagmire and it was decided to focus on broader activites.

The scope of activities performed and the need for a great deal of personalized service results in considerable diversity in the type of personnel employed by corporate hospitals. While one usually thinks of hospital employees in terms of doctors, nurses, and a broad spectrum of professionals, a very large percentage of employment is made up of nonprofessional personnel. In 1967 total employment in municipal hospitals was 33,082. Of this total, barely 3 percent represented physicians with an additional 3 percent being residents. The largest single occupational category was nurses aides at 24 percent while all other nursing categories accounted for yet another 24 percent. Occupational therapists comprised 2 percent, dietary, institutional, and housekeeping aides 22 percent, and clerical and related positions 9 percent. In addition, there were 529 elevator operators, 716 laundry workers, 504 motor vehicle operators, 207 maintenance men, and 337 cooks. This is not an exhaustive list of occupations, but does give some indication as to the variety of employment within corporate hospitals.[1] According to records of New York City's Department of Personnel, hospital employment has remained at roughly the same level, approximately 37,000, in both 1960 and 1970.[2]

The seemingly small number of physicians can be accounted for by the affiliation system, under which all but two of the nineteen HHC hospitals are affiliated with either a voluntary hospital or a medical school. An affiliation agreement typically requires the affiliate to provide certain personnel to a municipal hospital covering broadly defined services, for which HHC covers payroll costs and partial overhead.[3] As of 1972 affiliate personnel agreements were largely restricted to physicians, thus, accounting for the low percentage of employment in the physician category. Unfortunately, the number of physicians made available to HHC hospitals each year under affiliation agreements could not be determined.

While it is reasonably simple to define primary and supportive functions of hospitals, available data can only approximate the measurements one would like.

[c]See Charles Brecher, *Where Have All the Dollars Gone?* (New York: Praeger Publishers, 1974), for additional detail on hospital operations in New York City.

To indicate gross medical attention rendered to patients, we use the number of patients served. Proxy measures used for primary activities are average daily census[d] (total days of patient care divided by 365) and admissions. These data are then disaggregated by major treatment category such as general, psychiatric, and tubercular care. In addition, ambulatory care (outpatient and emergency room) is also considered a primary activity with the number of visits to these departments serving as measures of their activity level.

Use of average daily census and admissions as proxies in measures of the number of patients served may seem initially to be somewhat redundant but there are differences in interpretation. Average daily census does indeed satisfactorily reflect the number of patients receiving treatment. An admission, however, reflects two factors: turnover, showing new people entering for care, and an indirect measure of the specialized and heightened activity one experiences upon admission. That is, when first admitted more medical service is likely to be administered to a typical patient than later on in hospitalization; the latter part of the stay is often structured more around rest, recuperation, observation, and follow-up treatment. More laboratory tests, x-rays, and examinations generally occur during the first few days of stay than subsequently. Thus, use of admissions here is looked upon as general indicator of those medical services for which more detailed data could not be compiled.

In terms of support activities, the only direct measure available is laboratory tests performed. Average daily census, however, does allow us to make some general inferences about supportive services such as provision of food and linen. We may assume, in general, that each patient receives three meals a day plus a change of linen. Thus, simply knowing the number of patients under care gives a rough indicator of the volume of housekeeping support entailed.

Activity and Performance[e]

On an average day in 1973, there were 10,832 patients in HHC hospitals, around 22 percent less than in 1966[4] (see Table 6-1). Every category of care shown had some reduction in average daily census except drug-addiction treatment, which went up 219 percent between 1967 and 1973. However, with only 137 patients on an average day, this type of care represents a very small segment of overall hospital activity. The largest decrease occurred in the area of tubercular care (67%), while the smallest was for general care (10%). Thus, it would appear that specialized care has diminished much more rapidly than general care while, on the whole, there were far fewer patients in 1973 than in 1966. The peak year for average daily census was 1966, for every category except drug-addiction treatment, when nearly 14,000 patients were served per day.

[d]One can easily obtain total patient-days of care by multiplying average daily census by 365. Activity indexes for the two series will be identical.
[e]Detailed data by year and borough are contained in Appendix A, Tables A-42 to A-45.

Table 6-1
Health and Hospital: Activity Indicators

Indicator	Amount (1973)	Index (1966 = 100)	Peak Amount	Peak Year
Primary Activities				
Average daily census:				
All inpatients[a]	10,832	78	13,956	1966
General care	6,443	90	7,191	1966
Psychiatric care	1,050	78	1,350	1966
Tubercular care	407	33	1,274	1967
Newborn nursery	356	77	465	1966
Chronic and extended care[b]	2,304	70	3,272	1966
Drug addiction	137	319[c]	168	1972
Admissions:				
All inpatients[a]	248,267	98	263,064	1971
General care	218,077	105	230,842	1971
Psychiatric care	25,467	73	34,885	1966
Tubercular care	2,483	63	3,961	1966
Newborn (births)	24,069	66	36,577	1966
Chronic and extended care[b]	4,125	108	4,125	1973
Drug addiction	2,310	263[c]	4,142	1971
Ambulatory-care visits:				
Emergency room	1,708,462	113	1,708,462	1973
Outpatient department	4,798,856	141	4,798,856	1973
Supportive Activities				
Laboratory tests:				
All inpatients	19,729,913	198	19,729,913	1973
Outpatients	9,706,681	343	9,706,681	1973

[a]The categories listed below are selective and do not add up to total inpatients amounts.

[b]This category encompasses related categories that have been called by a variety of names over the study period, including: chronic care, extended care, custodial care, skilled-nursing care, and health-related care.

[c]The index numbers for drug-addiction treatment are based on 1967 = 100.

Source: Hospital Statistics Service, *Statistical Profile: NYC-Corporate Hospitals*, 1966-70 and 1969-73 (New York: Health and Hospital Corporation, no date, mimeographed).

Number of admissions has not fallen off nearly as sharply as average daily census (implying, in general, a shorter length of stay). Total admissions went down just 2 percent between 1966 and 1973, to 248,267; this is, however, a decrease of almost 15,000 over the peak found in 1971. Admissions for general care did rise during the study period, although the categories that decreased slightly outweighed it. General-care admissions increased 5 percent; drug-addiction admissions 163 percent; and chronic and extended-care admissions[f] 8 percent. Admissions in this latter category had fallen at first, but then began to increase again between 1972 and 1973 (from 2,890 to 4,125) indicating a possible renewed demand for long-term care. Drug-addiction treatment showed by far the largest relative gain in patients admitted during the study period, although 1973 admission (2,310) fell far below those in 1971 (4,142). It is difficult to believe that this decrease manifests a general trend. There is no reason to assume that the need for this care has diminished, it seems rather that methods other than hospitalization, such as methadone programs, have become more favored treatment modes.

New admissions have declined the most for tubercular, newborn, and psychiatric care. In considering newborn care, it should be pointed out that "newborn admissions" are births. Thus, this measure manifests maternity and delivery-room activities. There were slightly more than 24,000 births in corporate hospitals in 1973, 34 percent fewer than in 1966, the peak year.

The final dimension of primary activity concerns ambulatory care. This is the only major category that experienced growth during the study period. Emergency room visits were up 13 percent and outpatient department visits 41 percent. In addition to these being the only major area of expansion, the sheer magnitude of activity within them is enormous. There were more than 1.7 million emergency-room visits and almost 4.8 million outpatient-department visits in 1973. These represent peak activity for both, suggesting continued growth is likely. The high level of activity for these departments is probably due to a phenomenon common to large cities. That is, the poor tend to use readily available facilities to compensate for their lack of money to pay for private physicians combined with a lack of physicians serving low-income areas.[5] Previously it was noted that the only supportive activity on which data were available is laboratory tests. In 1973 alone almost 20 million laboratory procedures were performed for inpatients, 98 percent more than in 1966. This is in sharp contrast to the absolute decline in volume of inpatients receiving care. It is apparent that the number of lab tests per patient has begun a sharp upward trend. In fact, when we divide the number of tests by the number of patients admitted, there are some 80 tests per patient. Relative growth in laboratory tests for outpatients rose even more than for inpatients (243%), reaching 9.7 million by 1973; there was an average of two tests per outpatient visit. While relative growth has been far greater for outpatient tests, the incidence per patient is far lower than for inpatients.

It was suggested earlier that we might infer the magnitude of certain support activities using average daily census. We can, therefore, assume that food and

---

[f]The latter, referred to by a variety of names during the study period, encompassed in 1973 chronic care, skilled-nursing care, and health-related care. Generally, it refers to long-term care, most often for the elderly.

linen services have decreased, on the whole by about as much the average daily census for inpatients (22%). Other supportive services, however, are not likely to be as closely linked to the number of inpatients; therefore, we cannot draw conclusions concerning their trends. If other medical support, such as x-rays, physical therapy, and pharmacy services, are related to inpatients in a manner similar to laboratory tests, then we might assume considerable upward change for them as well.

To summarize trends, it is clear that the average number of patients served in corporate hospitals each day has dropped sharply while at the same time the number of patients admitted has fallen only very slightly. There are exceptions noted for certain specific categories of care. A contrary trend is found for ambulatory visits, however, suggesting that HHC hospitals are increasingly serving the role of the private physician. While the number of patients under care has dropped it seems that the volume of treatment per patient may have increased, especially if other medical services follow the trend reflected by laboratory procedures.

Enactment of Medicare and Medicaid legislation may have had an impact on hospital use during the study period. Obviously the effect has not been an absolute increase in the use of HHC facilities on an inpatient basis, although it may have influenced outpatient usage. It seems at least plausible that poor patients might be diverted to nonmunicipal hospitals if they no longer had to worry about payment for services. This can be examined further in Table 6-2, which shows the percentage of total patients discharged by type of hospital ownership.

The level and distribution of discharges changed very little between 1965 and 1973. Proprietary, voluntary, and state hospitals had a slightly higher share, and corporate hospitals a slightly smaller share of patients discharged in 1973 than in 1965. By 1973 voluntary and state hospitals had gained 1 percent each at the

Table 6-2
Share of Total Patients Discharged by Hospital Ownership

| Year | Total Discharges | Percent of Total | | | |
		Voluntary Hospitals	HHC Hospitals	Proprietary Hospitals	State Hospitals
1973	1,192,766	63	21	15	2
1972	1,224,155	62	21	16	1
1970	1,155,961	62	21	15	1
1966	1,104,879	62	23	14	1
1965	1,117,761	62	23	14	1

Source: Health Facilities Data Informational Systems of the Health and Hospital Planning Council of Southern New York, Inc., *Hospital Statistics of Southern New York*, 1973, 1972, 1970, 1966, and 1965 (New York: no date).

expense of proprietary hospitals. It does seem evident that neither Medicaid nor Medicare have had a strong impact on relative use of hospital facilities. Although discharges in all hospitals grew 7 percent in the period 1965 to 1973, there was a rather erratic trend of increases and decreases throughout the period. In fact, hospital use actually showed a drop in the year between 1965 and 1966 when this legislation first went into effect. It may, de facto, have had considerably more impact on the use of physicians and nursing homes and could have contributed to a greater use of ambulatory-care facilities.

Shifting attention to performance, one encounters particular difficulty with respect to hospitals. Ideally, one would like to have a measure of "improved state of health" as a performance indicator; no such statistics exist either conceptually or operationally. The only available statistic that even approaches being an indicator of performance is the average length of stay. In using this measure one must assume that any lessening of average stay indicates that a hospital is now able to administer as much (or even more) treatment in a shorter length of time. Performance indicators are shown in Table 6-3.

Average length of stay has fallen for three of the functions under study, has remained the same for one, and has risen for two. An average stay for a general-care patient has fallen from thirteen to eleven days. This is a significant reduction (although far from the greatest), since the great bulk of the patient population falls within this category. A drop of one or two days when cumulated over tens of thousands of patients means a whopping savings in patient-days and financial expenditures. Length of stay for tubercular care has

Table 6-3
Health and Hospital: Performance Indicators

Indicator	Amount 1973	Index (1966 = 100)	Peak[a] Amount	Year
Average length of stay (days):				
General care	11	85	11	1973
Psychiatric care	15	107	14	1968
Tubercular care	58	52	58	1973
Newborn care	5	100	5	b
Chronic and long-term care	198	63	198	1973
Drug addiction	21	117[c]	14	1971

[a]In this case, the "peak" of activity is actually the shortest length of stay during the time period, not the highest.

[b]Length of stay has remained constant at five days.

[c]1967 = 100.

Source: Hospital Statistics Service, *Statistical Profile: NYC-Corporate Hospitals*, 1966-70 and 1969-73 (New York: Health and Hospital Corporation, no date, mimeographed).

been nearly halved from 1966 to 1973, from 112 to 58 days, but the patients involved number far fewer. Another area that showed heightened performance is chronic and long-term care, declining from 322 to 198 days. The average length of stay for newborns has remained unchanged at five days throughout.

Two areas that exhibited decreases in performance, as indicated by an increased average length of stay, were psychiatric care (from 14 to 15 days) and drug addiction (18 to 21 days). It should be noted that the length of stay for drug treatment has varied considerably between 1967 and 1973, ranging from 14 (1971) to 26 days (1969). These data may reflect an uncertainty about the appropriate length of time needed for drug addiction or psychiatric treatment.

Given the mixed trends in average stay, it is difficult to frame an unequivocal statement on performance. On the whole, however, it can be said that performance has improved since indicators for the major types of care show shorter lengths of stay. In fact, a two-day time saving cumulated over the 200,000-plus admissions in a year represents major savings of time and scarce medical resources as well as private expenditures.

In addition to the activity and performance indicators, we should also mention HHC endeavors under New York City's productivity program. Apparently this has been largely confined to administration and management such as reduced time for administrative functions and supply procurement; increased rate of bill collection; improved services and decreased costs in housekeeping, maintenance, linen, and dietary services; and assignment of nonnursing tasks to less skilled personnel. Other than reduced length of stay and increased number of ambulatory patients, the only productivity increase directly related to medical attention was a reduction in physician-response time to emergency calls by 50 percent.[6] While this is a dimension of concern, albeit hard to convert into quality of health, it does not impact on the great bulk of people served by HHC.

Conclusions

The general trend of inpatient activity (measured by admissions) has shown a slight contraction. However, admissions for general care, the major treatment category, rose slightly. Major reductions in activity have occurred in specialized areas such as psychiatric, tubercular care, and births. Significant upward change is noticeable in drug-addiction treatment although the number of patients this represents is a very small proportion of the total clientele. Although overall admissions have decreased only slightly, the average number of patients hospitalized at any time has decreased by much more, indicating a reduction in general levels of medical activity. Most pronounced growth in corporate hospital activity was found in emergency room and outpatient department care. Medical supportive activities, as indicated by laboratory tests, have also expanded greatly, in sharp contrast to the trend for patients served. Performance indicators present a more mixed picture, but overall we can say there was an increase in performance reflected by a two-day decrease in length of stay in the major treatment category, that which affected 218,077 patients in 1973, nearly 90 percent of all admissions.

Notes

1. Eleanor G. Gilpatrick and Paul K. Corless, *The Occupational Structure of New York City Municipal Hospitals* (New York: Praeger Publishers, 1970), p. 32.

2. City of New York, Department of Personnel, Civil Service Commission, *Annual Report* (New York: 1959 and 1969).

3. Citizens Budget Commission, Inc. *The New York City Health and Hospital Corporation* (New York: 1972), p. 39.

4. Unless otherwise indicated, statistics are taken or derived from: Hospital Statistics Service, *Statistical Profile: New York City–Corporate Hospitals*, 1966-70 and 1969-73 (New York: Health and Hospital Corporation, no date, mimeographed).

5. Citizens Budget Commission, Inc., *The New York City Health and Hospital Corporation* (New York: October 1972), p. 6.

6. City of New York, Health and Hospital Corporation, *Productivity Program* (New York: 1972), pp. 1-5.

7

Department of Sanitation

Overview

The Department of Sanitation (DOS), incorporated into the newly formed Environmental Protection Administration in 1968,[a] is charged with the following duties: sweep, clean and flush city streets; remove snow and ice; collect and remove refuse from residential, public, and special-use buildings; empty department litter receptacles; gather and remove fallen leaves; provide for cleanup of storm debris; remove street sweepings; provide for disposal of waste materials by operation, maintenance, and use of incinerators, truck landfills, and marine loading and unloading plants; reclaim waste swamplands for public benefit by landfill operations; repair and maintain equipment and machinery; and issue summonses and warnings for violations of the New York City Health and Administrative Codes.[1]

The volume of refuse generated in a city with the population of New York is gargantuan. A total of 9.1 million tons of refuse of all types (including demolition and construction waste, dead animals, and lot-cleaning residue) were received by the department for disposal in the single 12-month period between July 1972 and June 1973.[b] Nearly one-half of this was physically collected by DOS; other sources were private cartmen 11 percent, construction waste 36 percent, and government and charitable sources 4 percent. This differs quite a bit from 1960-61, when private cartmen supplied about 31 percent and construction waste 12 percent; DOS's share was slightly larger then at 54 percent. The biggest change has been a tripling of construction waste's share. Aside from refuse collection, there are nearly 12,000 curb-miles in New York City to be swept, flushed, cleared of snow and ice, or otherwise kept free of litter. These tasks were undertaken with a 1973 work force of 9,633 Sanitation men and another 1,597 DOS employees serving as superintendents, foremen, assistant foremen, etc.; both represent an 11 percent expansion of personnel over a 12-year period.

[a]Incorporation of the Department of Sanitation into the Environmental Protection Administration was largely an administrative consolidation; the duties of the department did not change.

[b]Department of Sanitation compiles its statistics on a fiscal-year rather than calendar-year basis. Unless otherwise noted, data are taken or derived from: City of New York, Environmental Protection Administration, *Annual Progress Report and Statistical Review of the Department of Sanitation* from July 1, 1960-June 30, 1961 through July 1, 1972-June 30, 1973 (New York: various years).

Analyzing the activities of the New York City Department of Sanitation is considerably easier than analyzing other city departments because its activities are more readily quantified. One can measure the amount of refuse collected and destroyed or the miles of city streets swept, plowed, or cleaned. These figures do not stand as proxies for nonquantifiable activities but are themselves of immediate concern. In addition, performance measures can be constructed from the data collected and reported by DOS. For example, we can consider information such as the number of man-days expended in collecting or disposing of a ton of refuse or compare the miles of street cleaned to total curb-miles in a sub-area of the city. The only nonquantifiable (and generally unavailable) performance measures in the area of sanitation are those elusive indicators for cleanliness. While we know what it is, it is very difficult to deal with since it is often more the absence of something than its presence.

For purpose of analysis, we consider all refuse collection, street cleaning (including sweeping, water flushing, and manual sweeping), snow-removal operations (including plowing and salt-spreading), and removal of abandoned vehicles as primary activities of DOS. Supportive tasks include disposal of refuse (including incineration, marine transfer, and landfill operations); maintenance of plant and equipment; and general administrative, training, and clerical functions. Supportive activity indicators are shown only as they relate to refuse disposal operations due to limitations on data availability.

Activity and Performance[c]

The magnitude of some operations of DOS is staggering. Refuse collected and destroyed is measured in millions of tons; streets swept in millions of miles and man-days and truck shifts in hundreds of thousands. Changes in primary and support activities of DOS are shown in Table 7-1 and are discussed below.

The sole indicator used for refuse-collection is the volume collected. This amounted to 3,902,096 tons in 1972-73, a 41 percent growth since 1960. The 1972-73 figure, however, reports a very slight drop (about 28,000 tons) for the first time after peaking in 1971-72. It is not possible to say whether this is a reversal of past trends but it does represent the first decline in refuse collected in over a decade.

The street-cleaning responsibility of DOS is effectuated through three main activities: street sweeping by power sweepers; flushing streets with water; and manual cleaning. The former two activities are measured in miles, the latter in man-days. Miles swept with power equipment rose over 78 percent between 1960 and and 1973 reaching 1,314,554. Miles flushed, on the other hand, fell 37 percent, to 272,868, while manual street cleaning likewise dropped (31%) to 106,874 man-days expended. Flushing activities had peaked back in 1960 and

[c]Detailed data by year and borough are contained in Appendix A, Tables A-46 to A-61.

Table 7-1
Department of Sanitation: Activity Indicators

Indicator	Amount (1972-73)	Index (1960-61 = 100)	Peak Amount	Year
Primary Activities				
Refuse collection:				
Tons collected	3,902,096	141	3,930,418	1971-72
Street cleaning:				
Miles swept (power sweeping)	1,314,554	178	1,314,554	1972-73
Miles flushed	272,868	63	430,200	1960-61
Manual cleaning (man-days)	106,874	69	160,354	1961-62
Snow and ice removal:				
Miles plowed per inch fall	112	3	3,485	1960-61
Miles of salt spread per inch fall	8,168	568	8,168	1972-73
Towing operations:				
Vehicles towed	695	5[a]	17,395	1966-67
Truck shifts	3,100	51[a]	7,799	1967-68
Supportive Activities				
Refuse disposal:[b]				
Total tons handled	9,108,599	155	9,108,599	1972-73
Incineration	1,390,771	81	2,325,253	1966-67
Truck landfill	4,834,250	223	4,834,250	1972-73
Marine transfer	2,881,731	146	2,903,131	1971-72

[a]The index numbers for towing operations are based on 1963-64 = 100, the first year for which data were available.

[b]These categories do not sum to total tonnage because the category "other disposal" is not shown separately.

Source: City of New York, *Annual Progress Report and Statistical Review of the Department of Sanitation*, July 1, 1960-June 30, 1961 to July 1, 1972-June 30, 1973 (New York: Environmental Protection Administration, various years).

manual cleaning in 1962, while power sweeping reached its peak in the most recent year. Thus, it becomes obvious that water flushing and manual-cleaning operations have long since peaked in importance and are being, de facto, slowly phased out. Power street sweeping has become the primary method for fulfilling the department's street-cleaning charge. It should be noted that the real advent of power sweeping occurred after 1970, with flushing and manual cleaning also showing a slight reversal of past declines during this period. Wider reliance on power sweeping seems a clear instance of a trade-off favoring less labor-intensive methods.

Another primary activity of DOS, albeit of a seasonal nature, is removal of snow and ice from city streets. The main methods for accomplishing this task are plowing and spreading salt and abrasives. These activities are measured in terms of miles plowed and miles of salt spread. To reflect this activity properly, however, one must take into account the amount of snowfall in a given year. To do this, these activity indicators were standardized for the amount of snowfall each year.

In 1972-73, 112 miles were plowed for each inch of snowfall, a 97 percent drop from 1960-61 when it stood at 3,485 miles plowed per inch. However, there was an extreme disparity in the total amount of snowfall in these two years. In 1960-61 there were 57.3 inches of snow compared with only 3 inches in 1972-73. It seems reasonable to assume that more clearing activity will be required for greater quantities of snowfall as there is likely to be a need for repeated plowing and salt spreading during a heavy snowfall while light falls can often just be left to melt. Therefore, a standardizing of these operations by the amount of snowfall does not completely neutralize the impact of weather variation. In spite of this, plowing activities have been markedly *less* in *every* year after 1960-61 than during that year. As an instance, take 1966-67 when 51.5 inches of snow fell, almost the same amount as the base year. In this year only 1,907 miles were plowed per inch of snowfall, somewhat more than half the plowing activity of the base year with roughly the same volume of snow.

A partial explanation for the decrease in plowing might be accounted for by the increase in a complementary activity, salt spreading. This activity has risen sharply (468%) between 1960-61 and 1972-73, to 8,168 miles per inch of snowfall. Salt spreading has been notably higher during the latter years of the study period. Thus, it appears that less expensive salt spreading has, somewhat at least, replaced more costly plowing activities, especially when snowfall is relatively light. Salting unlike plowing activities, however, are not entirely contingent on snowfall (i.e., salt can be spread for slippery conditions that do not involve snow). Therefore, part of the marked increase in salting may be attributable to a higher incidence of icy weather. In any event, it seems clear that some trade-off in activities has occurred with salt spreading replacing plowing, the former being a cheaper, faster, and easier means of dealing with bad road conditions.

A final activity considered as primary, is the department's removal of abandoned and/or derelict motor vehicles from city streets. The pattern of towing activities is measured by both tow-truck shifts and the number of vehicles towed. Number of vehicles towed decreased 95 percent between 1963-64 and 1972-73. In 1972-73 only 695 vehicles were towed as compared with 17,395 at the peak (1966-67). However, this is due mainly to the fact that beginning in 1967-68 DOS began a policy of having private contractors tow vehicles that the department had tagged for removal. Work under this program has expanded since that time and in 1972-73 about 76,000 cars were removed.[d] The other indicator, tow-truck shifts, fell off 49 percent over 1960-73 to 3,100 in the latter year. It is not completely clear why truck shifts have not decreased by as much as vehicles towed, but it is possible that tow trucks are being used to locate and tag vehicles for removal and thus are recorded in the same category as prior to the advent of private contract removals. Whatever the reason, cars towed per truck shift have plummeted since the peak of 2.6 to a dismal 0.22.[e]

For purposes of this study, refuse disposal is considered a support activity. Refuse received for disposal includes collection by DOS and private cartmen; construction, demolition, and lot cleaning waste; dead animals; and refuse from miscellaneous sources. In addition, waste is generated during the disposal process itself, for example, incineration residue that must be disposed of. During 1972-73 the department and miscellaneous sources accounted for 49.1 percent of all refuse received, licensed cartmen 10.8 percent, demolition and construction waste 36.3 percent, and government and charitable sources 3.8 percent. In 1960-61 DOS sources accounted for somewhat more, 54.2 percent, but private cartmen contributed a much larger proportion 30.7 percent, with construction and demolition wastes relatively light at 11.7 percent, and other sources at 3.4 percent.

Tonnage handled by all disposal methods has appreciated 55 percent between 1960-61 and 1972-73, reaching over 9.1 million tons. To accommodate this volume, there have been major shifts in disposal methods. Waste disposed of by incineration dropped 19 percent, while that going into truck landfill and marine transfer increased 123 and 46 percent, respectively. The peak year for incineration disposal was 1966-67, while truck-landfill and marine-transfer operations have peaked in the latter two years of the study. It appears that recent concern over environmental standards and the placement of DOS under the Environmental Protection Administration in 1968 has caused a shift in disposal operations away from incineration toward less (obviously) polluting alternatives.

It is possible to compute a variety of performance indicators due to the excellent statistical records maintained by DOS and the nature of its activities. Some activities may be analyzed in terms of man-days or truck shifts (these could also be considered productivity indicators, although this is not our immediate interest), some in the mileage of activity performed relative to total mileage. The performance measures discussed below are shown in Table 7-2.

Performance for refuse collection is shown by tons per man-day, which has

---

[d]This program has proved beneficial in another unexpected way: Due to higher prices for scrap metal, the city received up to $16.60 per car from contractors in 1974, whereas in 1973 it had to pay $10 per car for removal (reported in the *New York Times*, November 4, 1974).

[e]Even the peak of 2.6 vehicles towed per truck shift does not seem very high for a full shift of work. The current level of 0.22 raises some interesting questions as to what is done in these 3,100 truck-shifts expended.

Table 7-2
Department of Sanitation: Performance Indicators

Indicator	Amount (1972/73)	Index (1960/61 = 100)	Peak Amount	Peak Year
Refuse collection:				
Tons per man-day	3.31	125	3.31	1972-73
Street Cleaning:[a]				
Miles swept per total miles	113.40	146	113.40	1972-73
Miles flushed per total miles	23.50	52	45.10	1960-61
Snow and ice removal:[a]				
Miles plowed per total miles	0.03	b	20.99	1960-61
Miles salted per total miles	2.10	24	13.60	1966-67
Towing operations:				
Vehicles per truck shift	0.22	9	2.60	1968-69
Refuse-disposal operations: (Tons per man-day)				
Incinerator operations	10.10	116	10.40	1970-71
Truck landfill	102.40	213	102.40	1972-73
Marine transfer	101.20	154	101.50	1971-72

[a]Miles of street swept. flushed, plowed, or salted relative to the total number of miles in the city.

[b]Less than 1 percent.

Source: City of New York, *Annual Progress Report and Statistical Review of the Department of Sanitation*, July 1, 1960-June 30, 1961 to July 1, 1972-June 30, 1973 (New York: Environmental Protection Administration, various years).

risen some (26%) during the study period to 3.31. Street-cleaning performance is measured by computing the ratio of total miles cleaned (by various methods) to total mileage in an area (for example, curb mileage in a borough or all New York City). There was substantial growth in this ratio for sweeping (46%), with flushing performance declining about the same (48%). The peak year for sweeping operations was the last year of the study, while the peak was attained by flushing in the base year. This situation is undoubtedly due to the gradual phasing out of street-flushing activities in favor of the faster, cheaper, more efficient power-sweeping method.

Similar performance proxies are used for snow- and ice-removal operations. Miles plowed divided by total miles in area was only 0.03 in 1972-73, undoubtedly due to the extremely light snowfall in that year. The peak in performance for this activity was the base year, 1960-61, when each mile of street was plowed nearly twenty-one times. A somewhat different trend is manifest in salting operations, although it also decreased considerably. Each mile was salted approximately twice in 1972-73, as compared with almost fourteen times at the peak, 1966-67. However, when interpreting these data it should be remembered that they can be influenced by weather conditions as well as DOS operations.

Towing-operations performance is measured here by vehicles towed per truck shift. This has plummeted 91 percent between 1960-61 and 1972-73 to 0.22 vehicles per shift. In the peak year (1968-69), 2.6 vehicles were being towed per shift. In later years there seems to have been a considerable number of truck shifts that were *not towing any vehicles.* It was speculated previously that some truck shifts may be used to tag cars for removal by private contractors, which would tend to lower the performance indicator if both towing and tagging truck shifts are lumped together. At any rate, towing effectiveness has been decimated.

The final performance indicator is tons per man-day for various refuse-disposal operations. "Man-days" includes work performed by support as well as operating employees. Tons per man-day for incineration was 10.1 in 1972-73, a small fraction of that for either truck landfill (102.4) or marine transfer (101.2). This is due to the nature and relative scale of operations of each disposal method. However, in change terms performance increased the least for incinerator operation, 16 percent, and the most for truck landfill, 113 percent, with marine transfer rising 54 percent. Significantly greater reliance on the latter two methods for refuse disposal has been effectuated without comparable increases in manpower, thus the increased performance for these disposal techniques.

In addition to performance indicators calculated from department statistics, achievements under the New York City productivity program should also be noted. These have been of varying types, including improvements in support functions and management that have led to greater productivity or performance in primary functions. Among the accomplishments of this program were a new scheduling system, which arranged the off-duty days of sanitation men so that sufficient manpower was available to handle peak loads on Mondays and Tuesdays.[f] This reduced the need for night collection and associated overtime pay. New routes also have been arranged, which permit collection of more tons per shift as well as a reduction in shifts. Finally, there was a reduction of missed collections from 10 percent of scheduled collections in June 1969 to nearly zero in June 1973.

Improvements in the maintenance procedures for sanitation trucks have helped reduce the percentage of trucks out of service on any given day from 38 percent of the entire fleet in 1970 to about 10 percent in 1973. This has occurred largely through decentralized maintenance, setting of time standards for repair and maintenance work, and better inventory control over parts and materials.[2] Similar advances have been achieved for the repair of other DOS

---

[f]Accomplishing this seemingly simple feat actually took Mayor Lindsay nearly two years. See Andrew Hacker, *The New Yorkers* (New York: Mason/Charter, 1975).

equipment. In addition, older trucks are being replaced by larger trucks with almost the entire fleet scheduled for replacement by the end of 1973, thus offering the potential for even further gains in productivity.[3]

Conclusions

The general impression obtained from perusal of DOS activities is that there have been increases in general activity categories, although there have also been declines that are apparently associated with a shift in emphasis on the method for fulfilling particular tasks. The major function, refuse collection and disposal, has expanded steadily, while there has been a more recent emphasis on disposal methods other than incineration mainly in favor of truck landfill. Growth in all these activities has far exceeded growth in manpower.

It is less easy to discern an overall trend for other primary activities. As relates to the cleaning of streets, flushing and manual cleaning operations have decreased over 30 percent each and power sweeping rose 78 percent. While there have been fluctuations, it is safe to say that an average street gets more DOS attention now than in 1960-61. Less obvious, however, is the net effect on cleanliness. Snow and ice removal operations also exhibit a trade-off in methods used, with salting activities apparently replacing much plowing.

Trends in performance indicators are upward in almost all categories. Major growth has taken place in some refuse-disposal operations, while there have also been noticeable gains in refuse collection and street sweeping. The only declines as shown by the indicators used, are in those activities that are apparently being phased out or deemphasized, and in snow and ice removal, which is strongly affected by weather conditions. For the department as a whole, however, performance seems to have been on the increase over the 13-year period under study.

Notes

1. City of New York, *The City of New York Expense Budget for 1971-72*, (New York: undated), pp. 327-29.

2. Edward K. Hamilton, "Productivity: The New York City Approach," *Public Administration Review*, vol. 32 (November-December 1972), p. 789.

3. Herbert Ranschburg, Jonathan C. Dopkeen, and Roger Dreisbach-Williams, *New York City's Productivity Program: The Department of Sanitation* (New York: Citizens Budget Commission, 1974), pp. 9-24.

Part III:
Summary of Findings on
Output, Conclusions, and
Implications

8

Population and Public Services: Variation Among the Boroughs

Summary of the Determinants of Public Output

The potential for an association between population groups and the magnitude and extent of city service provision was introduced in Part I. This association is given closer scrutiny now with specific reference to several major population characteristics of the five boroughs that comprise the City of New York: Bronx, Brooklyn, Manhattan, Queens, and Staten Island.

A complete review of the literature that has developed concerning population characteristics and their relation to public service levels is beyond the intended scope of this study. Most work done in this area, however, has been concerned with an analysis of those factors that determine *dollar* expenditures by state and local governmental units. Although dollar expenditures on public service, per se, are not the focus here, it is generally recognized that higher levels of service (output) will be associated (probably closely) with greater dollar outlays. Therefore, any factors one can associate with expenditures may also be associated with public service activity.[a] Those population characteristics generally found to have been statistically related to the public services under study are summarized here, drawing on a past survey of this literature by Roy Bahl.[1]

Police Service

Nonwhite population and the density of population have often been found to be associated with additional need for police activity. Various studies of population characteristics and their relation to crime have found a positive association between the following groups and the level of crime: low income, unemployment, young males, and nonwhite population.[2] While crime itself is not of direct concern here, it is recognized that greater levels of crime generate greater demands for police output, certainly in the area of investigation if not also with patrol.

Fire Service

Both population density and the incidence of deteriorated housing have been found associated with fire services.[3] Although these are not, strictly speaking,

---

[a]Our concern is not dollars expended but the output or activity level of various departments under consideration. Refer to Chapter 1.

population characteristics they are reflective of a slum, ghetto-like environment and may therefore be associated with public service demands generated by a low-income concentration.

Sanitation Service

Few empirical analyses have dealt with the linkages between traits of the population and sanitation services. The only factors found to be associated with this public function have been density and high income.[4]

Hospital Service

Likewise, hospital service has not been subject to much analysis, possibly because it is related to the injured or ill, which are drawn from every population strata. However, more extensive use of hospitals has been attributed to the elderly.[5] Also, since we are studying city hospitals, their usage can clearly be linked to low-income groups since the primary purpose of the municipal-hospital system is to make available medical care to those whose income prevents them from obtaining private attention.

Social (Welfare) Service

Population groups associated with welfare activity can be identified by the eligibility requirements of public-assistance programs. The dominant trait is, of course, low or unstable income. Other characteristics also likely to be associated are old age, female-headed families, children under 18, and unemployment.

In summary, a great many population characteristics have been linked with one or more of the activities under study. Low income especially has been associated with many of these public services. Since the low-income population of large cities tends to draw very heavily from minorities, the black and Puerto Rican populations of New York City might be considered more closely related to several areas of public sector output.

Next we can turn to an analysis of the distribution of public services, as measured by major activities of the various departments, and the distribution of various population groups among the boroughs, in an attempt to determine whether features of the population have influenced public output in New York over the decade 1960-70.[b]

---

[b]The period 1960-70 is used to permit comparisons of output measures with population characteristics contained in the decennial census volumes.

Borough Population Characteristics

The first factor to be considered is the composition of each individual borough and any changes that have occurred between 1960 and 1970 (refer to Table 8-1). Although the population of the city as a whole altered only very slightly over these ten years (1.4%), population growth by borough varied much more widely. Brooklyn and Manhattan had drops in population (1.0 and 9.4%, respectively); the Bronx experienced a moderate increase (3.3%). At the other extreme, population in Queens rose nearly 10 percent while Staten Island experienced a proportionately explosive increase of one-third, but on a very small base. Much of the growth in Staten Island can probably be attributed to the opening of the Verezzano Narrows Bridge between Brooklyn and Staten Island in 1964; this established the first land link to the rest of New York City. This population growth should be kept in the context of relative shares. Staten Island has the smallest share (4%) and Brooklyn the largest (33%); the remaining three boroughs have similar population shares (19-25%).

In considering specific age groups, the number of children under 18 increased most in Staten Island (32.9%), just about the same rate as its total population growth. Patterns in the other boroughs were quite different. There was a major drop in the under-18 population in Manhattan (14.2%) and a relatively large increase in the Bronx (much larger than population change, 14.8%). Queens and Brooklyn had only moderate change in this group. Another age group of specific relevance is the elderly. Population over 65 rose almost 17 percent for the city as a whole and expanded in every borough. Manhattan showed the smallest increase (3.5%) while in Queens this group rose 42.1 percent. Changes in these two population groups—often labeled the more "dependent"—have been more pronounced than overall population movements.

The racial character of the city also has shifted drastically over the decade. With total population increasing by only 1.4 percent, the black population grew some 53.5 percent. The only recorded decline in this population group was found in Manhattan. Black population in the Bronx more than doubled (up 119%), while it increased between 60 and 80 percent in every other borough. The other dominant minority in New York City is the Puerto Rican population. Unfortunately, data on this group are not available for 1960. However, one can see from the 1970 distribution that high concentrations are found in the Bronx, Brooklyn, and Manhattan; these three boroughs also contain the heaviest incidence of black population. Nonwhite citizens are becoming more and more dominant in the city as a whole but it is especially pronounced in certain boroughs—Brooklyn, Bronx, Manhattan.

Certain other population groups are of interest and should be noted. Families with female heads went up in all boroughs (a range of 35-65%) except Manhattan, where it fell off slightly (4.5%). Young males (age 15 to 24) also rose

Table 8-1
Primary Population Characteristics by Borough: 1960 and 1970

Population Characteristic	Citywide	Borough				
		Bronx	Brooklyn	Manhattan	Queens	Staten Island
Total population ('000):						
1960	7,783 (100)[a]	1,425 (18)	2,628 (34)	1,698 (22)	1,810 (23)	222 (3)
1970	7,895 (100)[a]	1,472 (19)	2,602 (33)	1,539 (20)	1,985 (25)	295 (4)
% change	1.4	3.3	-1.0	-9.4	9.8	33.1
Population density (miles^2):						
1960	b	33,135	34,582	77,195	16,018	3,699
1970	b	35,895	37,172	66,923	18,393	5,095
% change	b	8.3	7.5	-13.3	14.8	37.7
Population under 18 ('000):						
1960	2,165 (100)[a]	405 (19)	785 (36)	386 (18)	512 (24)	77 (4)
1970	2,235 (100)[a]	465 (21)	816 (37)	331 (15)	520 (23)	102 (5)
% change	3.2	14.8	4.0.	-14.2	1.6	32.9
Population over 65 ('000):						
1960	814 (100)[a]	152 (19)	259 (32)	208 (26)	174 (21)	21 (3)
1970	948 (100)[a]	171 (18)	289 (31)	215 (23)	247 (26)	26 (3)
% change	16.5	12.2	11.5	3.5	42.1	24.8

Males 15-24 ('000):						
1960	456	92	164	89	97	13
	(100)ᵃ	(20)	(36)	(20)	(21)	(3)
1970	590	115	203	105	144	23
	(100)ᵃ	(20)	(34)	(18)	(24)	(4)
% change	29.4	24.7	23.7	18.2	47.5	74.3
Black population ('000):						
1960	1,085	163	370	396	146	10
	(100)ᵃ	(15)	(34)	(37)	(13)	(1)
1970	1,665	357	655	379	258	16
	(100)ᵃ	(21)	(39)	(23)	(16)	(1)
% change	53.5	119.1	76.9	-4.2	77.1	63.8
Puerto Rican population ('000):						
1970	812	317	272	185	33	5
	(100)ᵃ	(39)	(34)	(23)	(4)	(1)
Families with female head ('000):						
1960	269	49	88	79	48	5
	(100)ᵃ	(18)	(33)	(29)	(18)	(2)
1970	355	81	127	75	65	7
	(100)ᵃ	(23)	(36)	(21)	(18)	(2)
% change	32.1	65.9	43.9	-4.5	35.6	37.5
Low-income families ('000):						
1960	629	126	230	168	95	11
	(100)ᵃ	(20)	(37)	(27)	(15)	(2)
1970	528	126	200	106	85	10
	(100)ᵃ	(24)	(38)	(20)	(16)	(2)
% change	-16.1	0.5	-12.8	-36.6	-10.3	-13.9

Table 8-1 (cont.)

Population Characteristic	Citywide	Borough				
		Bronx	Brooklyn	Manhattan	Queens	Staten Island
High-income families ('000):						
1960	239	34	63	58	77	7
	(100)[a]	(14)	(26)	(25)	(32)	(3)
1970	405	53	104	84	136	18
	(100)[a]	(13)	(26)	(21)	(34)	(5)
% change	69.4	53.1	64.7	44.4	77.4	174.1
Unemployed in labor force ('000):						
1960	180	32	60	57	27	3
	(100)[a]	(18)	(33)	(32)	(15)	(1)
1970	139	23	47	35	31	3
	(100)[a]	(17)	(34)	(25)	(22)	(2)
% change	-22.6	-26.9	-21.6	-39.1	12.6	-3.6
Employed in labor force ('000):[c]						
1960	3,396	266	697	1,934	419	47
	(100)[a]	(8)	(21)	(58)	(12)	(1)
1970	3,100	234	548	1,724	428	51
	(100)[a]	(8)	(18)	(58)	(14)	(2)
% change	-8.7	-12.0	-21.3	-10.9	2.1	9.6
Housing units lacking plumbing facilities ('000):						
1960	176	9	48	101	15	2
	(100)[a]	(5)	(28)	(58)	(9)	(1)

1970	83	7	22	45	9	1
	(100)[a]	(8)	(26)	(53)	(11)	(2)
% change	−52.5	−21.2	−55.4	−56.0	−39.5	−41.1

[a]Figures in parentheses are the relative shares of the characteristic in each borough with New York City equal to 100 percent; they may not sum to 100 percent due to rounding.

[b]Not computed.

[c]Total employment can exceed sum of the boroughs since some persons did not specify their place of employment within New York City. Borough distribution is based on sum of reported employment in the five boroughs.

Sources: Population characteristics were taken or derived from: U.S. Bureau of the Census, *Characteristics of the Population*, vol. 1, pt. 34, New York, 1960 and 1970; housing characteristics were taken or derived from: U.S. Bureau of the Census, Census of Housing 1970, vol. 1, *Housing Characteristics for States, Cities and Counties*, pt. 34, New York; and U.S. Bureau of the Census, U.S. Census of Housing 1960, vol. 1, *States and Small Areas*, pt. 6; employment characteristics were taken from: U.S. Bureau of the Census, *Census of Population*, Subject Reports: *Journey to Work*, 1970 and 1960.

substantially in all boroughs (18-47%) but particularly in Staten Island (74%). Families with low income[c] declined in every borough (10-36%) except the Bronx where there was a less than 1 percent growth. The relative distribution of low-income groups may be of more import than any overall change, however. Although low-income families fell in absolute number in every borough except the Bronx, which had a considerable increase (4%) in its share of all the city's poor families, Brooklyn and Queens had very slight increases and Manhattan a substantial drop (7%). High-income families[d] increased significantly in all boroughs (44-77%) and more than doubled in Staten Island (174%). The number of labor-force members classified as being unemployed dropped in every borough except Queens where its growth exceeded 12 percent.[e]

Also related to income level is the presence of deteriorated housing[f] (since the census no longer reports this category, housing lacking plumbing facilities is used). A deteriorated housing stock may be considered representative of slum conditions and poverty in general. Deteriorated housing has fallen by large amounts in all boroughs (21-56%). The largest concentrations of such housing in existence in 1970 were in Manhattan, with more than one-half the city's total, and Brooklyn with another 26 percent.

Yet another population group to be considered is those persons employed within the city's border. Both resident and nonresident workers exert demands on city government, particularly for those services that relate to public safety, health, and transportation. New York remains a major commercial and financial center with a high level of employment even though overall employment within the city fell almost 9 percent over the decade; more than 3 million people continued to work in New York as of 1970. Employment rose in only two boroughs—Queens and Staten Island (2.1 and 9.6%); Manhattan alone accounted for 58 percent of all the city's jobs; Staten Island and the Bronx had relatively

[c]Low-income levels have been derived from the Bureau of Labor Statistics lower cost of living standard for New York City, modified to exclude taxes, medical expenses, work-related expenses, and school lunches. See Jean C. Brackett, "New BLS Budgets Provided Yardsticks for Measuring Family Living Costs," *Monthly Labor Review*, vol. 92 (April 1969), pp. 3-16. This has been used in place of federal criteria, which are believed to understate poverty. This lower standard of living amounted to $5,000 in 1967, which was adjusted to $4,500 for 1960, and $5,800 for 1970 by use of the (total) consumer price index. These amounts are for a family of four. However, due to limitations of census data used, all families earning less than these amounts are included in the lower income category here.

[d]Upper income families were determined in a similar manner using the Bureau of Labor Statistics higher budget for New York City. The 1967 budget of approximately $15,000 was adjusted to $13,300 in 1960 and $17,400 in 1970. Families earning more than these amounts were included in the upper income category.

[e]This situation has undoubtedly worsened since 1970 with the rising national unemployment rate and its tendency to hit hardest on inner-city, poverty-prone areas.

[f]This connection is made clear in Hugh O. Nourse and Donald Phares, "Socio-Economic Transition and Housing Values: A Comparative Analysis of Urban Neighborhoods," in G. Gappert and Harold Rose, eds., *The Social Economy of Cities*, vol. IX, Urban Affairs Annual Reviews (Beverly Hills, California: Sage Publications, 1975), pp. 183-208.

small shares. While the majority of those who work in the city also live in the city, almost one-fifth commuted in from outside city limits in 1970, compared with only about 15 percent in 1960. This reflects the trend toward decentralization of urban population.

In summary, relative to their share of total population, Queens and Staten Island had disproportionately higher shares of high-income families and lower shares of low-income families, combined with smaller shares of both blacks and Puerto Ricans. While Brooklyn had the largest population share, it had an even larger share of black and low-income families and a smaller share of high-income families. The Bronx and Manhattan fall in the mid-range—their shares of the black population are not much larger than of the total population. However, the Bronx had a much greater proportion of Puerto Ricans than total population, in addition to having more low-income families than might be expected and considerably fewer high-income families. In general, we can see that the Bronx, Brooklyn, and Manhattan exhibit similarities in containing the bulk of the lower income and minority populations, while Queens and Staten Island have larger shares of wealthier families and fewer minority group members. Both Queens and Staten Island did, however, increase in population more than other boroughs and both had significant growth in their black population, albeit from a much smaller base.

Borough Service Variations: A Statistical Perusal

The final stage of analysis focuses on variation in output of public services across boroughs and how it is influenced by the various population traits discussed above. Table 8-2 shows major activities of each department[g] for 1960 (or the earliest available year) and 1970, the change in each activity, and the relative share as distributed by borough.

It is clear from a simple scan of the data that there are significant differences both in the growth of activities and in their distribution among the boroughs. To substantiate this observation, a Chi-square test was performed both on the change in activity (1960-70) and on the 1970 distribution of activities. Results from the Chi-square analysis are provided in Table 8-3. Testing for changes in the activity level between 1960 and 1970 indicates that we can accept the hypothesis that growth in each borough was significantly different from the average increase for each activity at the 0.05 level. In other words, we can say that a different rate of increase for different activities is not a "statistical accident."

[g]Not all of the activity indicators available on a citywide basis were available for individual boroughs and the number available varies greatly by department. Therefore, one or two prime indicators have been selected for each service to simplify analysis and permit more consistent treatment. Measures selected are those most readily identifiable with the department's major responsibilities.

Table 8-2
Primary Activity Indicators by Borough: 1960-66 and 1970

Indicator	Citywide	Borough				
		Bronx	Brooklyn	Manhattan	Queens	Staten Island
Police Department						
Felonies investigated ('000):						
1966	304 (100)a	50 (17)	85 (28)	125 (41)	40 (13)	4 (1)
1970	489 (100)a	81 (17)	142 (29)	175 (36)	84 (17)	8 (2)
% change	60.8	61.7	67.1	39.9	108.1	89.9
Felony arrests ('000):						
1960	36 (100)a	5 (15)	10 (28)	15 (41)	5 (14)	b (2)
1970	94 (100)a	20 (21)	29 (30)	34 (36)	10 (11)	1 (1)
% change	163.9	270.5	184.2	128.9	113.7	124.2
Misdemeanors and violations investigated ('000):						
1960	302 (100)a	38 (12)	86 (28)	127 (42)	45 (15)	7 (2)
1970	678 (100)a	96 (14)	181 (27)	269 (40)	110 (16)	23 (3)
% change	124.2	154.9	109.5	111.9	145.9	219.5
Fire Department						
Fires extinguished ('000):						
1960	61 (100)a	13 (21)	19 (31)	15 (25)	11 (18)	3 (6)

1970	127 (100)[a]	31 (25)	45 (35)	27 (22)	17 (14)	6 (5)
% change	108.8	149.9	141.6	79.1	58.2	73.1
Nonfire emergencies ('000):						
1960	17 (100)[a]	2 (14)	6 (35)	5 (30)	3 (18)	b (2)
1970	46 (100)[a]	10 (21)	16 (34)	13 (27)	7 (15)	1 (3)
% change	172.6	301.1	162.5	147.8	128.5	205.7
<u>Department of Sanitation[c]</u>						
Tons of refuse collected ('000):						
1960	2,758 (100)[a]	439 (16)	921 (33)	601 (22)	693 (25)	105 (4)
1970	3,649 (100)[a]	666 (18)	1,132 (31)	727 (20)	956 (26)	167 (5)
% change	32.2	51.7	22.9	20.9	37.9	59.5
Street cleaning—miles swept ('000):						
1960	740 (100)[a]	98 (13)	246 (33)	230 (31)	131 (18)	36 (5)
1970	855 (100)[a]	132 (15)	295 (35)	299 (35)	115 (13)	14 (2)
% change	15.5	34.5	20.2	30.3	−12.1	−61.3
<u>Social Services[d]</u>						
Public-assistance cases ('000):						
1960	125 (100)[a]	24 (19)	42 (34)	50 (40)	7 (6)	1 (1)
1970	375 (100)[a]	69 (18)	147 (39)	94 (25)	62 (17)	4 (1)
% change	190.9	182.6	246.1	88.9	769.9	199.8

Table 8-2 (cont.)

Indicator	Citywide	Borough				
		Bronx	Brooklyn	Manhattan	Queens	Staten Island
Health and Hospital Services						
Admissions ('000):						
1966	254	54	78	84	36	2
	(100)[a]	(21)	(31)	(33)	(14)	(1)
1970	251	58	79	75	39	b
	(100)[a]	(23)	(31)	(30)	(16)	b
% change	-1.0	6.9	0.8	-11.2	9.2	-55.5
Ambulatory visits ('000):						
1966	4,904	1,290	1,449	1,577	588	0
	(100)[a]	(26)	(30)	(32)	(12)	(0)
1970	4,555	1,271	1,370	1,325	589	0
	(100)[a]	(28)	(30)	(29)	(13)	(0)
% change	-7.1	-1.4	-5.4	-15.9	0.2	0

[a]Figures in parentheses are the relative share of the characteristic in each borough with New York City equal to 100 percent; they may not sum to 100 percent due to rounding.

[b]Less than 1,000 or 1 percent, whichever is applicable.

[c]Based on a fiscal year rather than calendar year: 1960 = 1960-61, 1970 = 1970-71, etc.

[d]Data are for one month of the year (January 1970 and December 1960), representing an average monthly volume of cases.

Sources: Derived from New York City, Police Department, *Annual Report*, 1960-70 (New York: Printing Section, Police Department, City of New York, undated); and New York City, Police Department, *Statistical Report: Complaints and Arrests*, 1971-73 (New York: Office of Programs and Policies, Crime Analysis Section, Police Department, City of New York, December issues); Fire Department, City of New York, *Annual Report*, 1960-69; and *Annual Statistics*, 1970-72; City of New York, Human Resources Administration, *Monthly Statistical Report*, January 1960 through January 1974 (New York: no date, mimeographed); Hospital Statistics Service, *Statistical Profile: NYC-Corporate Hospitals*, 1966-70 and 1969-73 (New York: Health and Hospital Corporation, no date, mimeographed); Health Facilities Data Informational Systems of the Health and Hospital Planning Council of Southern New York, Inc., *Hospital Statistics of Southern New York*, 1973, 1972, 1970, 1966, and 1965 (New York: no date); and City of New York, *Annual Progress Report and Statistical Review of the Department of Sanitation*, July 1, 1960-June 30, 1961 to July 1, 1972-June 30, 1973 (New York: Environmental Protection Administration, various years).

Table 8-3
Chi-square Values for Selected Activity Indicators

Activity by Department	Calculated Chi-square[a]	
	Change in Activity (1960-70)	Distribution of Activities and Total Population (1970)
Police Department:		
Felonies investigated[b]	37.8[c]	17.0[c]
Misdemeanors and violations investigated	54.9[c]	25.9[c]
Felony arrests	128.6[c]	23.3[c]
Fire Department:		
Fires extinguished	71.9[c]	7.4
Nonfire emergencies	15.9[c]	6.9
Sanitation Department:		
Tons collected	29.5[c]	0.4
Miles swept	30.4[c]	18.9[c]
Social Services:		
Public assistance cases	979.8[c]	6.9
Hospitals:		
Admissions[b]	78.0[c]	9.9[c]
Ambulatory visits[b]	27.0[c]	14.3[c]

[a]Chi-square value at 0.05 level with 4 d.f. = 9.488 and with 3 d.f. (hospital activities) = 7.815.

[b]Change calculated over period 1966-70.

[c]Statistically significant at 0.05 level.

A similar test was performed on the 1970 distribution of activities compared with the 1970 distribution of population (see Table 8-3). The results of this test indicate that, at the 0.05 level, the borough distribution of most activities differs significantly from the borough distribution of population. The exceptions to be noted are fires extinguished, nonfire emergencies, tons of refuse collected, and public-assistance cases. With the exception of refuse collection, Chi-square values for these four activities are significant only at the 0.20 level. It appears that of all the activities under consideration, refuse collection is the one most directly linked to population per se.

As there appears to be substantial variation in both the distribution of service outputs and population groups, the next stage of analysis will determine whether these variations are associated. This will be done by use of the Spearman coefficient of rank order correlation (r_s). The borough distribution of activities (absolute *level*) and population groups in 1970 are ranked and tested by this method as will be ranked *changes* in activities and population groups between

1960 and 1970. Due to the small number of observation, at a 0.05 level, an r_s greater than 0.90 is necessary for statistical significance. In other words, nearly perfectly matched rank orders are required. However, since this study examines an entire population rather than a sample, the question of significance in the general statistical sense is not of immediate concern, that is, results from these tests are not to be inferred to a larger or different population. Therefore, we consider an r_s value of 0.90 or greater to be highly significant and those in the range 0.70-0.90 to be significant. Correlations for changes in activities and population groups are given in Table 8-4.[h]

In general, few clear associations were uncovered in the test applied to changes in outputs. Police operations—as reflected by misdemeanors and violations investigated—were associated with more population categories than any other activity. Increases in these investigations were associated with a change in population, density, young males, upper income families, and population under 18. The other police output variable examined, felony arrests, was related only to female-headed families. Change in Fire Department activities was linked to very few characteristics—an increase in fires extinguished was related to black population and unemployment while nonfire emergencies were associated with growth in female headed families and population under 18. Sanitation activities had a considerable number of significant (r_s) values. The change in tons of refuse collected was highly related to total population, density, population under 18, young males (the latter two may be spurious as there is no a priori basis for assuming these groups generate more trash than others), and also upper income families and deteriorated housing. One other Sanitation Department indicator— miles of street swept—was associated with unemployment although the reason why is unclear.[i] The final activity—public-assistance cases—was highly associated with unemployment and less strongly so with the elderly population. It also was related to upper income families, although this seems likely to be spurious.

Although an analysis of the *change* in activities and population traits exposed some associations there were very few considering the number of variables tested and the potential relations one might anticipate based on the extant literature on this topic. Some population groups showed little or no linkage to *any* public sector activity. As an example, take low-income families, which one would expect to be related to growth in several public-sector activities but was, in fact, related to none.

The same test applied to 1970 distribution (*levels*), however, uncovered far more associations, many at a highly significant level (see Table 8-5). In addition, a number of other variables that were not considered in the "change" test due to

[h]Only those activities for which data were available in 1960 and 1970 were used for this test.

[i]It may be that unemployment (and poverty) leads to a higher tendency toward loitering and deteriorated neighborhood conditions, thereby affecting the volume of trash that accumulates on the streets.

Table 8-4
Spearman Coefficient of Rank Correlation for Changes in Activities and Population Groups: 1960-70

Population Characteristics	Felony Arrests	Misdemeanors & Violations Investigated	Fires Extinguished	Nonfire Emergencies	Tons of Refuse	Miles Swept	Public-assistance Cases
Total population	-0.50	0.86[a]	0.40	0.60	0.90[a]	0.30	0.50
Density	-.50	-.86[a]	.40	.60	.90[a]	.30	.50
Males 15-24	-.50	-.86[a]	.40	.60	.90[a]	.30	.50
Black population	.55	.13	.70[a]	.40	.35	.35	.40
Low-income families	.30	.30	.30	.30	.40	.30	.40
High-income families	.60	.73[a]	-.60	.00	.70[a]	.40	.70[a]
Unemployment	-.60	.50	-.70[a]	-.30	.50	-.80[a]	.90[a]
Female-headed families	.70[a]	.34	.60	.80[a]	.50	.30	.10
Population under 18	.10	.80[a]	.20	.80[a]	.90[a]	-.30	.10
Population over 65	-.60	.55	-.60	-.10	.65	-.60	.70[a]
Deteriorated housing	.10	.55	.50	.40	.70[a]	.10	.30
Employment	-0.80[a]	.60	-0.80[a]	-0.20	0.50	-0.70[a]	0.10

Note: Decreases were treated as negative increases and ranked as follows: the smallest decrease was equivalent to the largest increase.
[a]Indicates a highly significant relationship ($r_s \geq 0.90$) or significant relationship ($0.90 > r_s \geq 0.70$).

Table 8-5
Spearman Coefficient of Rank Correlation for 1970 Distribution of Activities and Population Groups

Population Characteristics	Felonies Investigated	Felony Arrests	Misdemeanors & Violations Investigated	Fires Extinguished	Nonfire Emergencies	Tons of Refuse	Miles Swept	Public-assistance Cases	Hospital Admissions	Ambulatory Visits
Total population	0.60	0.50	-0.10	0.60	-0.60	1.00[a]	0.60	0.70[a]	0.70[a]	0.40
Population over 65	.60	.50	-.10	.60	-.60	1.00[a]	.60	.70[a]	.70[a]	.40
Population under 18	.35	.30	-.50	.70[a]	-.30	.90[a]	[b]	.60	.60	.20
Density	.95[a]	1.00[a]	.30	.70[a]	-.20	.50	.95[a]	.90[a]	.90[a]	.80[a]
Black population	.85[a]	.90[a]	.10	.90[a]	-.10	.70[a]	.95[a]	1.00[a]	.90[a]	.80[a]
Puerto Rican population	.45	.60	-.50	.90[a]	.40	.30	.65	.70[a]	.70[a]	.70[a]
Female-headed families	.60	.70[a]	-.30	1.00[a]	.20	.60	.80[a]	.90[a]	.90[a]	.80[a]
Low-income families	.60	.70[a]	.30	1.00[a]	.20	.60	.80[a]	.90[a]	.90[a]	.80[a]
High-income families	.45	.30	.20	.30	-.80[a]	.90[a]	.35	.45	.45	.40
Males 15-24	.35	.30	-.50	.70[a]	-.30	.90[a]	.45	.60	.60	.60
Unemployment	.85[a]	.80[a]	.20	.70[a]	-.50	.90[a]	.85[a]	.90[a]	.90[a]	.90[a]
Deteriorated housing	.95[a]	.90[a]	.40	1.00[a]	-.60	.70[a]	.85[a]	.65	.65	.60
Borough employment	0.95[a]	0.90[a]	0.40	1.00[a]	-0.60	0.70[a]	0.85[a]	0.65	0.65	0.60

[a]Indicates a highly significant relationship ($r_s \geq 0.90$) or a significant relationship ($0.90 > r_s \geq 0.70$); $r_s = \pm 1.0$ means identical rankings.
[b]Not tested.

a lack of data for 1960 can be tested now (especially hospital outputs). Two additional population categories are also included: the Puerto Rican population and borough employment. The latter variable is of interest since it is recognized that transients as well as residents can exert demands on the city.

Analysis of the 1970 distribution of Police Department activities uncovers some conflict with earlier findings. Felony investigations and arrests are related to several population variables, although misdemeanor and violation investigations are not significantly related to any. This is a reversal of the Spearman correlation results for increases in police activities. Those variables most closely associated with both felony arrests and investigations are population density, black population, deteriorated housing, and employment. The latter is likely to be spurious as we have no reason to postulate any direct relationship between employment and major crime. Unemployment was related to both investigations and arrests while female-headed and low-income families were related to arrests. With the exception of employment and female-headed families, all variables noted above have been found to be associated with police output or crime in the literature surveyed. The only variable that, it was anticipated, would be related to police activity but was not found to be was young males. Several of those variables found significant are closely tied into low income and may, in fact, be better and/or broader indicators of poverty than the actual income measures themselves.

Turning to Fire Department activities, we found a situation similar to that for police, that is, one activity (fires extinguished) is related to most population traits, while the other (nonfire emergencies) is related to only one, high-income families. In this instance, fires extinguished is related to ten of the thirteen variables examined, although it is acknowledged that some of these may be spurious; this can be contrasted with the results of the correlation analysis of changes in activities where fires and emergencies were related to just two variables. Fires were most closely linked with low-income and female-headed families, deteriorated housing, employment, and both black and Puerto Rican population. Less close associations were found for density, population under 18, unemployment, and young males. All of the variables that one would expect to be related to fire service are included—most particularly poor-quality housing and low-income. Borough employment seems a spurious association, as we have no a priori basis for associating it with a higher incidence of fires.

Sanitation services manifest a number of strong linkages with population groups. As forewarned by the literature, refuse collection was closely associated with higher income families and total population but not with density. It was also related to the under 18 and over 65 age groups, young males, unemployment, and black population. Street sweeping was most closely related to density, unemployment, deteriorated housing, and black population and less so to employment, low income, and female-headed families. Thus, this service appears to be rather clearly linked to poverty.

The rank order of public-assistance cases and hospital admissions was identical in 1970; therefore, they are related to the same population variables. This is not surprising, in as much as the city hospital system exists largely to serve those who cannot afford private care. As might be expected, most of the poverty indicators are also associated with these measures, including low income, female-headed families, unemployment, and black and Puerto Rican population. Other related variables are population over 65, density, and total population.

Conclusions

Generally speaking, findings from these statistical tests indicate that the distribution of different population subgroups was linked to the distribution of many public service activities in 1970, while the *change* in these activities was less frequently associated with changes in population characteristics. It appears that population composition is far from the sine qua non of the operations of a New York City department. This was particularly evident with police and fire where many significant relationships were found for one or two activities but none at all for others. This implies that one cannot infer that *all* services of a department are affected by the same variable(s) found to affect *some* of its activities.

Many associations between activities and population subgroups expected on the basis of past analysis were also found to hold in New York City. In particular, some or all of the population characteristics related to poverty (e.g., female-headed families, black population, unemployed, and deteriorated housing) were found to be associated with most of the activities considered. It is interesting to note that one of the city's large minority groups—the Puerto Rican population—was related to only four activities, although three of these can be considered poverty related. Other variables found significant in several cases were density, total population, employment, and the elderly. Based on these, admittedly tentative, findings, it seems reasonable to conclude that variation across boroughs in the level of public activity has been influenced by various population groups within each borough but that other factors also play an important role. Furthermore, additional detailed study of the effect population mix and its change has on output levels is needed and would be an extremely worthwhile focus for future research.

Notes

1. Roy Bahl, "Studies on Determinants of Public Expenditures: A Review," in Selma G. Mushkin and John F. Cotton, eds., *Functional Federalism: Grants-In-Aid and PPB Systems*, (Washington, D.C.: State-Local Finances Project of the George Washington University, 1968), pp. 184-207.

2. President's Commission on Law Enforcement and Administration of Justice, *The Challenge of Crime in a Free Society* (Washington, D.C.: U.S. Government Printing Office, 1967), p. 5; Belton J. Fleisher, "The Effect of Unemployment on Juvenile Delinquency," *Journal of Political Economy*, vol. 71 (December 1963), pp. 543-55; John P. Allison, "Economic Factors and the Rate of Crime," *Land Economics*, vol. 48 (May 1972), pp. 193-96.

3. Edward H. Blum, *Urban Fire Protection: Studies of the Operations of the New York City Fire Department* (New York City: New York City RAND Institute, January 1971).

4. The Urban Institute, *Measuring Solid Waste Collection Productivity* (Washington, D.C.: June 1972), p. v.

5. Ronald G. Ehrenberg, "The Demand for State and Local Government Employees," *American Economic Review*, vol. 63 (June 1973), p. 374; Barbara S. Cooper and Nancy L. Worthington, "Age Differences in Medical Care Spending, Fiscal Year 1972," *Social Security Bulletin*, vol. 36 (May 1973), p. 9.

New York City's Fiscal Plight: Crisis of the Local Public Sector?

Review of Findings on Output and Performance

That the output of public services in New York City has risen is a fact beyond dispute. Data on expenditure trends attest to this, growth in employment attests to this, and, more importantly for this study, actual measures of output examined for five departments clearly attest to this. Indexes of activity discussed in each of Chapters 3 to 7 reveal marked shifts for nearly every facet of output considered. Perusal of data contained in Appendix A[a] enables one to follow these trends more closely, year by year, and, in the case of select major indicators, by borough as well. No matter where attention is focused, the most striking fact that emerges is the magnitude of expansion in operations in conjunction with the level of activity to which this growth applies. Levels of municipal activities are everywhere measured in units of tens or hundreds of thousands or even millions, with increases recorded over the period studied quite often exceeding 100 percent and in some instances reaching 500 to 1,000 percent or even more.

When "performance" is considered, the picture is far from one of ubiquitous improvement or increase. More often than not, measures of performance reveal a steady deterioration rather than an advancement, or at best very little improvement.[b] It seems that an expansion in services has very seldom become manifest as an improvement in those dimensions associated with better performance. Certain few gains have been made but they do not define the overall environment for municipal operations.[c]

Scrutiny of the data on output and performance suggests that three types of forces are in operation. Each of these can be viewed as a manifestation of the financial pressures that confront the City of New York. They also suggest the longevity of these fiscal tensions. First, while there has been unequivocal growth in the output of services as they relate to most primary departmental responsibilities, there are numerous instances of "cutbacks" or a "phasing out" of certain supportive or specialized services and even some primary activities. Second, as the data contained in Appendix A show, there has also been some reallocation of

[a]Appendix A contains data on each measure discussed in Chapters 3-7, broken down by borough as data sources permit.

[b]This is even more true when one relates the trend in performance to the relative importance or impact of the activity to which it applies.

[c]Perhaps most notable are sanitation (see Table 7-2) and length-of-stay for hospital care (see Table 6-3).

resources among the five boroughs. This has undoubtedly occurred in response to a greater need (perceived or real) in certain areas but it indicates that resources could not be increased everywhere.[d] Finally, in the trade-off between output and performance, the latter has emerged the loser on nearly every occasion. This suggests that "more" and "better" could not be achieved simultaneously, given the resources available.

These three forces are at least consistent with the hypothesis that financial constraints were eliciting alterations in the mix and spatial composition of public services and overall performance even during the heyday of expanding budgets, rising employment, and increased quantity and scope of programs. Also it is consistent with the argument of E.S. Savas that New York has assumed the status of a gigantic municipal monopoly providing many essential services. As this position was approached there was less and less concern over cost, output, performance, and accountability. As is true of most monopolies, inefficiency became the rule. Unique to "municipal monopolies," however, is a seeming lack of control over the perverse course of events that the city adhered to.[1]

Before delving into the concatenation of issues surrounding New York's plight, it is useful to review the findings on output and performance from Chapters 3 to 8. It is these data that bear witness to the current financial crunch of the New York fisc.

Police Department

Of the 37 measures of output for the Police Department[e] *only one* has exhibited any drop over the entire period 1960-73. Every facet of police operations has shown pronounced upward movement, whether it be of a primary, specialized or supportive nature.[f] Most often growth has exceeded 100 percent and in several (albeit less significant) instances has been in excess of 500 percent.

Performance seems to have followed a trend aimed in just the opposite direction. Clearance rates have *fallen* consistently for *every* category of crime over the full thirteen years studied, often by significant amounts. Recovery rates for stolen property have manifest an even more severe downward trend. It appears then that increases in NYPD activities have not been associated with any betterment of performance but have simply attempted to keep pace with criminal behavior.

---

[d]Manhattan, for example, has always been the beneficiary of the cleanliness provided by the Department of Sanitation's street sweeping and flushing activities, even at the expense of other boroughs. Undoubtedly, this is due to Manhattan's visibility to "outsiders." Some boroughs have received increased poverty-related services as their population mix evolved. Data in Appendix A enable these trends to be followed.

[e]Refer to Tables 3-1, 3-2, and A-1 to A-23.

[f]One must keep in mind the use of dual base years in examining "overall" trends.

Fire Department

Activity trends for fire operations[g] are somewhat more mixed. Every one of the nine primary measures rose, with a range between 34 and 555 percent. Looking at the volume and consequence of the tasks entailed underscores the impact of these relative expansions. As an example, false alarms skyrocketed by a factor of 6.5 to 1 and now nearly equal actual fires in occurrence. Support activities underwent pretty much the reverse trend for all but three of the ten dimensions looked at. Fire prevention endeavors seem on the way to extinction while investigations have plummeted and arrests nearly tripled. In terms of the consequence of occurrences, output in the fire department has unequivocally risen. As relates to preventive programs and investigations the evolution has been much less favorable.

Social Services

Operations coming under the rubric social services[h] have shown what can only be called explosive growth since 1960. Of the seventeen indicators considered, twelve have risen, with a range of increase between 14 percent and 422 percent. The greatest expansion, however, has been in those categories that exert the most pronounced impact fiscally. AFDC cases have risen 422 percent to a current level of nearly one-quarter of a million. Home relief and aid to the disabled also show major growth and number in the tens of thousands of cases. The only areas where a downward trend is noted are adult-shelter care and dental care, two of the less consequential involvements of DSS.

Performance for DSS is more difficult to evaluate, as has been noted in Chapter 5. Total cases closed, the measure reported on, has shown a sharp rise but those closed due to employment have fallen drastically for every category of welfare assistance. The number of cases involved in closings of all types remains a very small proportion of the overall level of welfare cases handled, less than 5 percent of the total. Cases closed due to employment has shown a steady decline and affects much less than 1 percent of all cases.[i] While there has been some improvement in performance, as proxied by case closings, the great bulk of the case load remains unaffected.

Health and Hospitals

Of the five major functional areas examined, health and hospitals[j] is the only one that has consistently had a falling level of primary activities. Out of the

[g]Refer to Tables 4-1 and A-24 to A-33.
[h]Refer to Tables 5-1, 5-3, and A-34 to A-41.
[i]This is a better but far from an ideal dimension of performance.
[j]Refer to Tables 6-1, 6-3, and A-42 to A-45.

sixteen facets recorded, ten have fallen, many by considerable amounts. Those that have risen are associated with treatment for drug addiction or ambulatory care, with only one exception. Along the major dimensions of average daily census and admissions, indexes have dropped 22 percent and 2 percent respectively. Steady growth was found in the areas of ambulatory care and supportive services such as laboratory tests. This generalized drop in output has become manifest as excess capacity in the corporate hospital system. The occupancy rate has continued to fall and is now at 77 percent, fully 10 percent or more below that existing in private facilities.[2]

Performance, as reflected by average length-of-stay, has shown improvement with an average stay now lower in every category except psychiatric and drug addiction. In weighing the impact of a two-day shorter stay for general care, affecting tens of thousands of persons each year the savings in time and resources are significant. It is, of course, difficult to know whether to attribute the improvement to HHC performance, per se, or the state of medical know-how. Undoubtedly, there is considerable interdependence between the two.

Sanitation

Sanitation operations[k] also have experienced an upward trend, but not along every facet examined. Refuse collection, street sweeping, and the spreading of salt have risen considerably while the remaining indicators have shown a decline. Disposal operations have kept pace with collections, as one might expect. There is also some improvement in performance for major DOS functions. These take on even more interest when one considers that employment for DOS has only gone up by 6 percent and expenditures by 61 percent between 1960 and 1973 as compared to the huge increases found for almost every other department (refer to Table 2-2).

In keeping matters in perspective, however, it should be noted that the responsibilities of DOS are probably much more amenable to advances in productivity, mechanization, and larger scale operation than are the more directly people-oriented and unique events encountered by the other four departments (e.g., fires, crime, illness, and poverty). Advances, however, do seem to be taking place, keeping firmly in mind the fact that the cost of municipal refuse collection exceeds $40 per ton compared to less than one-half that for private collection in New York and other cities.[3] Advances in productivity still remain firmly within the context of Savas' municipal monopoly.

---

[k]Refer to Tables 7-1, 7-2, and A-46 to A-61.

Municipal Output and the Population

That increased levels of public services are a function of a city's population seems almost self-evident. This is only a part of the picture, however. Two things are of note here: First, it is not growth in population, per se, that has exerted an upward force on municipal output in New York; *population has not risen between 1960 and 1973.* Rather, it is an altered composition of the population toward a more poverty-prone, dependent status that seems to have given rise to the rapid and significant shifts. This is especially evident in the areas of social services and health care. Second, there are a great many other forces at work to increase output, expenditures, and employment in the city than just its populace. This was partially substantiated in Chapter 8, which looked at the association between departmental output and a variety of population characteristics. It was found that some municipal service levels were not associated with any features of the populace. Police and fire operations can be attributed to a number of factors such as congestion and density and the externalities that they tend to generate,[1] as well as a more prevalent incidence of fires in lower income neighborhoods, and the tendency for more crimes to be reported the more police there are on the streets. Whatever the concatenation of forces in operation, it is more than just the population qua population of New York that has inflated output levels. A city's population is far from the sine qua non of municipal activity.

Evolution of New York's Fiscal Plight

Cries of a budget crunch emmanating from New York's City Hall sound a familiar refrain. In July 1932 Mayor James J. Walker warned of pending financial "embarrassment, if not a defunct condition."[4] Knowledge of the financial history of New York reveals that today's problems are not entirely new, just much more intense and less promising of any immediate resolution short of bankruptcy, default, or massive external help than in the past. How the situation reached the current crisis status is a question worthy of attention. There is, of course, no prime cause for New York's plight but rather a complex mixture of forces all pushing in the same direction.

Provision of Public Services

One factor that emerges is an expansion of municipal services, employment, and expenditures along virtually every possible dimension. A plethora of new

---

[1]Baumol has suggested that externalities may rise exponentially with population, for example, with the square of population rather than in proportion to it.

programs have been put into effect and old ones have been improved on and expanded. In addition, the city has been the source of staggering amounts of public construction such as bridges, tunnels, parks, and low- to middle-income housing.[m] Many of the services provided by the city are those not usually a municipal responsibility. For example, the corporate hospital system with a bed complement over 10,000 is a county function in most areas. This will claim $304 million or, along with other health care, $1.1 billion in fiscal 1975-76. City University of New York absorbs another $595 million to provide higher education to its 265,000 students—tuition free. Social services now exceed the budget for education and cost out at yet another $3.4 billion. Admittedly, the cost of these programs is shared with federal and state governments but a great deal remains a burden on the local tax base—23 percent or nearly $1 billion just for welfare.[5] Part of the problem is that past largesse by the federal government and New York State has backfired. A large portion of the growth in municipal operations was tied into the availability of "outside" funding for a variety of health, social service, and urban development programs. These have tended to get locked into the budget and then expand at a faster pace than external funding.[n] They also tend to generate indirect fiscal consequences. Net results: municipal New York was left holding the fiscal bag, partly out of greed, partly because the financial ground rules changed, and partly because the programs were successful in meeting the needs of an increasingly indigent citizenry. Much of the city's budget now pertains to items that are relatively "uncontrollable." Cutting back on any of them once they have been in effect is a most difficult task, one that has yet to be meaningfully confronted. A long tradition of offering extensive public services, the lure of matching funds for an array of state and federal programs, and the city qua county status all have contributed to the extreme scale of municipal expenditures.

Employee-Union Pressure

A second source of tension relates to the public employee-productivity-union nexus. "Baumol's disease" warns of the potentially dire fiscal impact on cities of sustained low productivity.[6] Taken in conjunction with a high rate of inflation, the financial effect is devastating. New York City seems to be one exemplification of Baumol's disease. Low worker productivity, especially vis-à-vis the private sector, permeates municipal operations and interacts perversely with inept municipal management. Endeavors to improve on productivity often require gargantuan outlays of time and effort to overcome union-worker

---

[m]See Robert Caro, *The Power Broker* (New York: Vintage, 1975), for a minute history of public works in New York City as implemented by Robert Moses.

[n]Martin Rein and Hugh Helco, "What Welfare Crisis?" *Public Interest*, no. 33 (Fall 1973), pp. 61-83, mention this with respect to social services. Other areas of similar impact include housing, transportation, and health programs.

resistance just to achieve minimal gains. Blatant cases in point are attempts to reschedule sanitation workers to meet peak-load collections, placement of additional patrolmen on the streets during high-crime periods, and maintenance and repair of DOS vehicles. It often took months, even years, to effectuate reasonably simple, basic, and obvious productivity enhancement measures due to the staunch resistance on the part of employees and their unions and the ineptness of the city bureaucracy.

Union and employee demands have made a severe financial dent in the city's resources in other, more immediately pecuniary, ways. Past handling of unions has resulted in some of the most generous labor settlements on record. These are a few notable examples: Bus drivers get paid time and one-half for time they do not work during the midday lull in traffic; policemen get four weeks vacation after one year on the job; donating a pint of blood earns the balance of the day off "to rest up"; a subway coin charger earns $229 per week; teachers receive $1 per day (on top of all other benefits) for every day worked until they retire.

On top of all this, as the capstone to city-union negotiations, are the pension plans. It has been projected that the cost of the various contributions the city makes to these programs could reach $2 billion per year if made actuarially sound. The provisions, de facto, are such that an employee can retire at nearly full pay after twenty years on the job by just putting in appropriate overtime during the last year of work. The full extent of all these provisions comes into focus when one considers Savas' argument that there is little effective demand for productivity or payment in accord with work performed due to the monopoly nature of municipal provision of services. The perverse twist here is that everyone winds up a scapegoat and no one a culprit.[7]

Tax-base Erosion

Another set of forces having its effect on the city is that pertaining to decentralization-recession. This impacts on the tax base, shrinking it, and adds demands for more of the expensive social and health services. During the decade 1960-70 the city's population had virtually stabilized; since then data suggest that population has fallen by several hundred thousand or about 4.2 percent. The pattern for employment has been similar. Jobs had been rising slightly up to 1970 but since then there has been nearly a 10 percent loss, some 369,000.[o] Businesses, people, and jobs have all been responding to the rather generalized forces of decentralization.[p] The economic environment has been further

[o]Robert D. Reischauer, "New York City's Fiscal Problem," Background Paper No. 1 (October 10, 1975), Congress of the United States, Congressional Budget Office (Washington, D.C.: U.S. Government Printing Office, 1975), table 4, p. 11. Other data sources imply that the employment loss may be even greater.

[p]Generalized in the sense that it has had at least some influence on most central cities, most especially, it seems, on the older, eastern cities.

worsened by the high taxes that are imposed on both business and people. Property taxes, a wide variety of business taxes, and a high sales and local income tax all have provided reinforcement to out-migration.[q] The problem, of course, with losses of people and business, is that the tax base has been shrinking relative to rapid growth in revenue requirements. Further reinforcing the needs-resources gap is the loss of the city's middle- and upper income families. These are the people most able to exit. Left behind are the lower income, poor, and indigent, with their need for costly municipal services and smaller base of taxable resources. While the better off pack their tax base and head for the suburbs, often continuing to work in the city, the fiscal capacity of the city to keep pace deteriorates.

National economic conditions have dealt yet another blow to the city's fisc. Heavy reliance on the sales and income tax in New York makes its tax structure cyclically responsive. So, as the economy advances, revenues make similar gains. Just the reverse prevails when economic conditions slow down, as has been the case for the past few years. Income and sales tend to drop off, affecting city revenues accordingly, and more and more people become eligible for social and health services. Resources contract at the time when services move upward in response to a larger indigent population.

The throes of decentralization place more attention on the need for some form of metropolitan or regional government better equipped to deal with the unique situation in the tristate area for which New York City is the employment and business core. While it serves the states of New York, New Jersey, and Connecticut, many have argued it does not get adequately compensated for its share of the financial responsibility. As far as the recession is concerned, New York is but one of thousands of governments suffering from its consequences. It does, however, help to spell out their inferior fiscal status in the federal system. Local government has precious little, if any, flexibility in confronting revenue losses suffered during a prolonged economic slump. They face constraints from all sides—taxpayers, the state, and threats of further loss of people and business if they raise taxes and the same if they do not maintain services.[r] Such a milieu leaves little room for creative, responsive local government. Instead it tends to conjure up an overwhelming sense of powerlessness and dependence.[8]

---

[q]The current property tax rate is over $8 per $100 assessed valuation with delinquencies running at 7 percent or about $220 million per year; the sales tax is now 8 percent; the city income tax has a rate structure that tops at 2 percent; and business is subject to a wide variety of taxes, such as business income, stock transfer, hotel occupancy, commercial rents, and financial corporations, to mention a few.

[r]The political sensitivity of tax increases has been quite convincingly demonstrated in Donald Haider and Thomas Elmore, Jr., "New York at the Crossroads: The Budget Crisis in Perspective," *City Almanac*, vol. 9, no. 5 (February 1975), p. 6. They show that there have been no major new city taxes enacted in a citywide election year or state taxes in a statewide election year.

The Debt Crunch

The catalyst for New York's precarious stance on the verge of default or bankruptcy is its inability to obtain absolutely essential funds from the municipal bond market. For a variety of reasons, culminating in a severe lack of investor confidence, New York City has not been able to sell bonds on its own since March 1975. Revenues planned on from the sale of bonds and notes, however, were vital for meeting municipal expenditures.[s]

The city's borrowing needs emmanate from three sources: First, capital projects are financed with long-term, predominantly "full-faith and credit" bonds, of which there are $9.4 billion outstanding. Short-term "bond-anticipation notes" are issued to cover costs in the initial stages of construction. Often, however, these notes have not been converted into long-term securities but just "rolled over." They now amount to $1.6 billion and the city had planned to issue $2 billion in new capital-related obligations and roll over $1.2-1.8 billion in outstanding notes. Second, to match the dissynchronous flow of revenues and expenditures, "tax- and revenue-anticipation" notes are issued. About $1.5 billion of these notes were to have been issued and paid off during fiscal 1975 in order to keep revenues in pace with expenses. Finally, short-term debt has been issued to cover perennial annual budget deficits. More than $2.5 billion such debt, representing the past decade's accumulated budget deficits plus $726 million for the current year, was to have been rolled over in fiscal 1975. New York City, therefore, had anticipated selling some $8 billion in municipal securities to meet revenue needs for fiscal 1975-76. As of April 1975, however, the city's capacity to enter the securities market was brought to a screeching halt. Absolutely mandatory revenue that was to have been derived from the sale of securities was not forthcoming and default or bankruptcy emerged as the most likely prospect.

All of this took place even with efforts on the part of New York State to carry the city over the immediate cash flow crunch. The Municipal Assistance Corporation (MAC) was established on June 10, 1975 to transform the city's short-term debt into long-term obligations. In spite of the moral obligation backing of the state and unprecedented tax-exempt interest rates up to 11 percent, "Big MAC" could not meet its charge. By September it, too, was unable to obtain any underwriting commitment. On September 9, 1975 the Financial Emergency Act (FEA) was signed by Governor Carey. It was the next step in a series of financial machinations to stave off default. This stopgap, emergency plan has encountered most of the same problems and resistance as MAC and seems unlikely to be able to keep the city solvent.

[s]Reischauer, "New York City's Fiscal Problem," offers an excellent overview of the debt crunch the city faces and its background. This section draws from this source.

On October 17, 1975 New York City was within minutes of default, with its bills exceeding revenues by $711 million.[9] Default was averted only at the very last minute by a reaffirmation to purchase $150 million in MAC bonds by the trustees of the United Federation of Teachers pension fund. This completed FEA's financial package to cover October's deficit. The scenario is far from played out, however, as New York City faces huge cash deficits every month through May of 1976–these total $6 billion.[10] The time table for default now seems to be set for November or December at the latest, unless there is external help.

Fiscal Gimmicks and Financial Wizardry

Another aspect of New York's fiscal plight is the heavy past reliance that has been placed on "gimmicks" and financial chicanery to achieve a "balanced budget." While one cannot dispute these machinations were successful in a very immediate, narrow sense, they seem to have had an overall detrimental impact on fiscal integrity and have probably helped cast the current image of the city in the eyes of investors, bankers, taxpayers, and state and federal policy makers. The long-term harm may well prove (if it has not already) to more than offset any short-run pecuniary gains. Dick Netzer has characterized the budget as a "fake piece of paper from the start of the fiscal year," a document that is *traditionally* surrounded with confusion, inadequate knowledge, obscurity, and stealth.[t]

While one cannot lay blame for the extant situation on these financial moves alone, there seems little doubt that they have seriously undermined confidence in virtually every phase of municipal finance. Perhaps of most crucial concern is access to the securities market for vital revenues. The following is but a partial listing of some of the gimmicks employed.[11] It is meant to be suggestive of the nature and extent of what has been taking place for years. It should also be noted that New York State was a covert accomplice in much of what went on: first, by allowing these fiscal gimmicks to be carried out, often in opposition to state law; second, by allowing an inappropriate division of responsibility to weigh too heavily on the local fisc.

Current year expenses were pushed into the next fiscal year, for example, $150 million in payrolls payable on June 30, 1975 were put off until July 1, 1975, the following fiscal year.

Pension plans for city employees are seriously underfunded. This is accomplished by using a 1914 actuarial base for projecting costs. It has been suggested that by 1977 there will be no assets to cover the liabilities for benefits earned by active members.

[t]Steven R. Weisman, "How New York Became a Fiscal Junkie," *New York Times Magazine* (August 17, 1975), p. 71, reports on Netzer's comments.

Revenues from the following fiscal year are included in the current year. To do this the city would borrow against federal and state aid, and sales and property tax revenues anticipated due during the next fiscal year, this, in spite of the fact that (1) often the aid would never materialize or had already been received, (2) delinquency rates on property tax collections are the highest since the Depression and now amount to 7.2 percent or about $220 million, or, (3) revenue earmarked to pay off borrowing already had a series of claims against it.

Proceeds from long-term borrowing for capital projects were used to cover current expenses. Apparently, this has exceeded $700 million in recent years.

In spite of state law nominally mandating a balanced expense budget, New York City has managed to accumulate about $3.0 billion in short-term debt issued to balance the budget over the past decade. Some $726 million was needed for the current fiscal year alone.

As municipal borrowing accumulated it was necessary to "roll over" debt coming due. Continual rolling over has precipitated a volume of municipal debt that currently exceeds $13 billion and claims $1.6 billion for debt service, 17 percent of the total city budget and nearly one-third of local tax receipts. New York City municipal debt now amounts to about $1,700 per capita as compared with a little over $2,000 for all outstanding federal debt.

As the debt crunch became more pressing all manner of devices were employed to have municipal securities bought by banks, pension funds, investors, and private citizens. Quite often tactics bordering on bribery and coercion were employed.

Last, there is the recent financial wizardry surrounding the Municipal Assistance Corporation and the Financial Emergency Act. Their purpose has been to carry New York City through the immediate crisis, keep it solvent, and buy enough time to implement the draconian cuts required to bring the budget truly in balance.

After just a cursory review of the steps taken to finance the city, it seems little wonder that Steven R. Weisman has characterized New York as a "fiscal junkie" everywhere seeking out another "revenue fix."[12]

Dealing with the Problem

In closing, it is appropriate to mention briefly what seems to be the range of alternatives within reason to ameliorate New York City's fiscal situation.[13] There are two temporal dimensions to the problem that must first be noted: One focuses on the very immediate deficit problem. The other addresses long-run solutions to the situation rather than further stopgap gimmicks and financial chicanery.

Over the next several months the city will face cash needs of the following amounts (in millions).[14] In 1975:

December $ 975

In 1976:

January	$1,377
February	621
March	1,029
April	154
May	57
June	+158 (surplus)

Not until June of 1976 is a surplus anticipated. Ceteris paribus, it seems inevitable that there will be a sequel to Friday, October 17 in each of these months until default becomes reality. The question is: what can be done to avoid default? The answer seems to be: nothing, short of immediate assistance on the part of the federal government. To avoid default the city either has to raise somehow billions of dollars in needed revenue through the sale of municipal securities or receive comparable amounts of outright cash assistance or loans. Nothing the City of New York can do *by itself* can possibly raise revenue or restore investor confidence quickly enough to cover the cash deficits over the next few months. Be that the case, and in the absence of federal "assistance," default is a certainty.

In the longer run, the options available are more plentiful and somewhat less painful. Table 9-1 outlines major policy steps that could be adopted to deal with the city's plight. Whatever the final collection decided upon, it is evident that services are going to have to be curtailed and perhaps eliminated in certain areas. They cannot possibly attain the projected levels shown in Table 9-2. Just how and where the cuts will occur remains to be worked out. It also is highly probable that a greater sharing of the cost of the expensive health, education, and welfare programs will be forthcoming. New York State's Home Relief Program and CCNY are obvious immediate sources of hundreds of millions of dollars in relief. The turmoil in New York City will at least help to bring into better focus the inappropriate division of responsibility that has become a financial albatross around the neck of local government.

Is New York City's Experience Generalizable?

For the most part, the city's experience is not generalizable. While it faces problems confronted by all local governments, it is differentiated along many critical dimensions. The scale of municipal operations, its unique financial and commercial status, its role as a point of entry for millions of immigrants to the United States, and its long tradition of liberal, expensive public services all have placed an extraordinary burden on the local tax base. Combined with the cumulative impact of the vast array of financial gimmicks it was allowed to induge in, most especially the issuance of municipal securities, it assumes a

Table 9-1
Policy Alternatives for New York City's Fiscal Plight

Level of Government	Policy Alternative[a]
City:	Reduce service levels
	Eliminate programs
	Raise existing fees and charges
	Raise tax rates
	Place greater reliance on fees and charges
	Eliminate exemptions, deductions, and "tax-exempt" status
	Implement management reforms
	Tie wages to productivity
	Eliminate reliance on fiscal "gimmicks"
	Avoid lure of federal-state largesse
State:	Provide greater direct state aid
	Realign division of responsibility between state and local governments
	Promote establishment of a metropolitanwide level of government
	Guarantee municipal securities
Federal:	Provide greater federal aid
	Make direct cash loans
	Provide federal "guarantee" of municipal securities financial integrity
	Realign division of responsibility among federal/ state/local governments
	Mandate local government restructuring
	Encourage Federal Reserve System involvement

[a]These are not mutually exclusive, nonoverlapping options.

somewhat unique status among American cities. This is not to say that other major core cities could not wind up in a similar predicament, just that it is unlikely that they would encounter a similar scale of severity. Perhaps default or bankruptcy (actual or imminent) in the world's wealthiest city will do for local finance and intergovernmental fiscal relations what Watergate has done for national politics, that is, at least raise an awareness of the problems and expedite a search for solutions rather than palliatives.

Table 9-2
Projected New York City Expenditures for 1979
(Millions)

Function	Slow Growth[a]	Percent of 1972 Level	Present Trend[b]	Percent of 1972 Level
Police	$ 880	147	$ 1,232	206
Fire	385	143	527	195
Environmental Protection Administration	428	152	606	215
Social Services Department	4,147	204	6,422	316
Health Services Administration	583	287	1,048	516
Public Schools	2,754	144	3,810	199
Higher Education	1,021	274	2,198	591
Total expense budget[c]	$13,452	158	$18,936	223

[a]Assumes one-half the present trend–1965-72 rate of increase.

[b]Based on the trend between 1965 and 1972.

[c]Includes more than the seven functions listed above.

Source: Roy W. Bahl, Alan Campbell, and David Greytak, *Taxes, Expenditures and the Economic Base* (New York: Praeger Publishers, 1974), tables 3.30-3.39. Refer to pp. 238-50 for detail on the methodology used.

Notes

1. E.S. Savas, "Municipal Monopoly," *Harper's* (December 1971), pp. 55-60.

2. "How to Save New York," *Time*, October 20, 1975, p. 15.

3. Ibid. or Citizens Budget Commission, Inc., *New York's Productivity Program: The Department of Sanitation* (New York: March 1974), p. 27.

4. See "Mayor's Pay-Cut Speech in 1932 Echoes Hauntingly," *New York Times*, August 1, 1975.

5. Robert D. Reischauer, "New York City's Fiscal Problem," Background Paper No. 1 (October 10, 1975), Congress of the United States, Congressional Budget Office (Washington, D.C.: U.S. Government Printing Office, 1975), table 6, p. 13.

6. William Baumol, "Macroeconomics of Unbalanced Growth: The Anatomy of Urban Crisis," *American Economic Review*, vol. 57 (June 1967), pp. 415-26.

7. Savas, "Municipal Monopoly."

8. See Norton Long, "Have Cities a Future?" *Public Administration Review*, vol. 33 (November-December, 1973), pp. 543-52.

9. "If New York Goes Bust," *Newsweek*, September 15, 1975, pp. 27-29.

10. Ibid., p. 27.

11. Compiled from various sources including: Steven R. Weisman, "How New

York Became a Fiscal Junkie," *New York Times Magazine* (August 17, 1975), p. 71; Reischauer, "New York City's Fiscal Problem"; and various recent issues of *Time, Newsweek, Business Week*, and the *New York Times.*

12. Weisman, "How New York Became a Fiscal Junkie."

13. See also the discussion in Attiat F. Ott and Jang H. Yoo, *New York City's Financial Crisis* (Washington, D.C.: American Enterprise Institute, 1975) and Joint Economic Committee, U.S. Congress, "New York City's Financial Crisis," (Washington, D.C.: U.S. Government Printing Office, 1975).

14. Ott and Yoo, *New York City's Fiscal Crisis*, p. 11.

Postscript

After completion of this manuscript in late October 1975, events affecting the New York City financial crisis took a major turn. On October 17, 1975 the city narrowly averted default as a commitment from the teachers' retirement fund was reaffirmed by its trustees. At that time it was anticipated the timetable for default had been put off until November or early December at the very latest. Somehow the cash deficit for November was covered and financial obligations were met. There was no way, however, short of massive external assistance that December's deficit of nearly $800 million could be covered.

After repeated statements to the contrary, President Ford announced federal intervention to help New York City deal with its short-run cash flow problem. On November 26, 1975, Ford made public plans to provide $2.3 billion in seasonal federal loans to the city to carry it over monthly deficits. Until such time as a combination of tax increases and budget cuts could be implemented and generate a surplus, these funds could be drawn on, up to a maximum of $2.3 billion per year, over a period of three years.

While undoubtedly the federal loans will cushion the severity of the immediate crisis, one still wonders as to its long run efficacy. New York has implemented major budget cuts, restructured its debt, frozen wages, and is in the process of making pension and management reforms. All of these steps are necessary and yet all are painful to residents and workers in a city accustomed to a "land of plenty." In addition, there is the pressure of cuts in services, programs, and benefits in the face of even higher municipal taxes. What the net impact on the budget will be remains to be seen. There is little question that the federal monies have provided breathing room for New York state and city officials to get their fiscal affairs in order. The immediate battle appears to have been won but the outcome of the war remains somewhat in doubt.

Appendix A:
Detailed Data on Public
Output and Performance
in New York City

The tables that follow provide data on all the output and performance measures discussed in Chapters 3 to 7, by year. In addition, many of the more significant ones have been compiled on a borough basis as well as citywide. To facilitate defining trends, these data have all been referenced to a base year, thus being converted into simple indexes of output and performance. The base amount of activity is shown to indicate the level of output as well as time trends over the period examined. The "high" level of activity for each measure is set in bold face, the "low" is set in italic. When a tie occurs, the latest year is so marked.

In the case of much of the Police Department data, dual base years had to be used due to the change in criteria for crime reporting adopted in 1966. Thus, between 1960 and 1965, 1960 = 100; between 1966 and 1973, 1966 = 100.

For several of the measures, the first or last year reported varies. This is due to (1) a phasing in or out of various programs, (2) statistical peculiarities in the data, or (3) the fact that the data were not available or did not exist. As many of the peculiarities of the data as are necessary for their proper understanding and use are noted on the appropriate tables in each chapter. It is hoped that the data contained in this appendix will make the study of even more use to those interested in changes in the output and performance of New York City, both in the aggregate and by borough. Sources of the data contained in these tables are as follows:

Police Department (Chapter 3)

New York City, Police Department, *Annual Report* (New York: Printing Section, Police Department, undated), for years 1960 to 1970.
New York City, Police Department, *Statistical Report: Complaints and Arrests* (New York: Office of Programs and Policies, Crime Analysis Section, December issues), for years 1971 to 1973.

Fire Department (Chapter 4)

Fire Department–City of New York, *Annual Report*, for years 1960 to 1969.
Fire Department–City of New York, *Annual Statistics*, for years 1970 to 1972.

Social Services (Chapter 5)

Human Resources Administration, *Monthly Statistical Report* (New York: City of New York, Human Resources Administration, undated), January 1960 to January 1974. Prior to the establishment of HRA, these were issued by the Department of Social Services.

Health and Hospital (Chapter 6)

Hospital Statistics Service, *Statistical Profile: NYC-Corporate Hospitals* (New York: Health and Hospital Corporation, undated), for years 1966 to 1973.

Department of Sanitation (Chapter 7)

City of New York, Department of Sanitation, *Statistical Review and Progress Report* (New York: Department of Sanitation, Bureau of Administrative Services, undated), for years July 1, 1960-June 30, 1961 to July 1, 1972-June 30, 1973.

Table A-1
Police Department: Crime Investigation—Total Felonies by Borough

Year	Citywide	Borough				
		Manhattan	Bronx	Brooklyn	Queens	Staten Island
1973	138	109	155	137	198	257
1972	137	114	157	135	181	208
1971	168	142	182	174	214	199
1970	161	140	162	167	208	190
1969	143	125	140	150	183	146
1968	137	126	146	142	150	129
1967	122	120	117	125	131	109
1966	100	100	100	100	100	100
Base (1966)	304,156	124,839	50,130	84,832	40,242	4,113
1965	153	146	186	148	154	166
1964	139	135	155	135	144	146
1963	123	122	138	120	121	119
1962	113	113	126	108	112	99
1961	105	106	111	101	101	96
1960	100	100	100	100	100	100
Base (1960)	108,491	47,723	14,027	31,653	13,581	1,507

Note: 1960 and '66 = 100. Dual base years used; refer to Chapter 3.

Table A-2
Police Department: Crime Investigation—Murder, Manslaughter, etc. by Borough

Year	Citywide	Borough				
		Manhattan	Bronx	Brooklyn	Queens	Staten Island
1973	230	236	311	196	194	250
1972	231	237	325	188	215	125
1971	200	192	275	183	175	125
1970	158	143	193	161	152	150
1969	153	152	171	153	134	100
1968	128	112	145	124	138	50
1967	103	98	121	104	89	100
1966	100	100	100	100	100	100
Base (1966)	683	252	140	216	67	8
1965	157	127	333	155	133	160
1964	160	151	250	158	133	120
1963	137	127	210	145	104	60
1962	127	120	188	120	118	160
1961	122	128	167	118	73	100
1960	100	100	100	100	100	100
Base (1960)	435	198	42	139	51	5

Note: 1960 and '66 = 100. Dual base years used; refer to Chapter 3.

130

Table A-3
Police Department: Crime Investigation—Rape by Borough

Year	Citywide	Borough				
		Manhattan	Bronx	Brooklyn	Queens	Staten Island
1973	171	160	197	157	202	240
1972	150	148	160	137	175	212
1971	111	122	111	94	126	136
1970	108	101	108	106	141	152
1969	109	110	107	109	111	100
1968	99	96	105	97	107	72
1967	105	108	101	96	125	140
1966	100	100	100	100	100	100
Base (1966)	2,180	761	431	734	229	25
1965	121	105	163	129	100	133
1964	116	104	156	117	100	120
1963	99	89	124	103	87	87
1962	101	98	103	103	108	87
1961	93	95	88	94	93	127
1960	100	100	100	100	100	100
Base (1960)	1,296	518	204	411	148	15

Note: 1960 and '66 = 100. Dual base years used; refer to Chapter 3.

Table A-4
Police Department: Crime Investigation—Assault by Borough

Year	Citywide	Borough				
		Manhattan	Bronx	Brooklyn	Queens	Staten Island
1973	105	91	124	107	126	135
1972	101	84	117	109	110	112
1971	88	77	96	98	89	87
1970	90	76	103	102	90	83
1969	85	73	98	96	77	72
1968	85	74	101	96	69	76
1967	108	99	118	113	113	99
1966	100	100	100	100	100	100
Base (1966)	23,204	9,375	4,277	7,136	2,154	262
1965	148	137	170	156	146	137
1964	135	130	146	134	140	158
1963	118	115	125	117	122	158
1962	113	113	117	109	113	126
1961	109	112	100	106	115	88
1960	100	100	100	100	100	100
Base (1960)	11,021	5,062	1,718	3,005	1,130	106

Note: 1960 and '66 = 100. Dual base years used; refer to Chapter 3.

131

Table A-5
Police Department: Crime Investigation—Robbery by Borough

Year	Citywide	Manhattan	Bronx	Brooklyn	Queens	Staten Island
				Borough		
1973	309	207	267	350	553	569
1972	332	293	310	365	506	569
1971	378	343	326	438	537	465
1970	315	293	265	352	464	326
1969	251	254	199	281	291	264
1968	231	229	228	235	239	243
1967	153	153	140	161	158	164
1966	100	100	100	100	100	100
Base (1966)	23,539	10,844	5,118	5,552	1,921	104
1965	135	131	163	137	109	188
1964	121	126	145	111	101	110
1963	104	105	117	98	95	124
1962	101	107	111	94	83	76
1961	91	94	93	91	75	107
1960	100	100	100	100	100	100
Base (1960)	6,579	2,854	988	1,941	755	41

Note: 1960 and '66 = 100. Dual base years used; refer to Chapter 3.

Table A-6
Police Department: Crime Investigation—Burglary by Borough

Year	Citywide	Manhattan	Bronx	Brooklyn	Queens	Staten Island
1973	125	102	136	114	188	208
1972	124	113	131	111	169	164
1971	151	141	161	147	177	157
1970	152	152	148	147	164	181
1969	143	142	133	141	165	146
1968	145	149	148	137	146	131
1967	125	134	115	120	128	106
1966	100	100	100	100	100	100
Base (1966)	119,783	43,590	21,486	37,450	15,241	2,016
1965	142	131	210	129	134	190
1964	127	119	162	121	127	165
1963	119	116	145	113	116	130
1962	115	114	144	104	121	110
1961	107	106	130	99	111	96
1960	100	100	100	100	100	100
Base (1960)	35,236	12,795	4,656	12,966	4,220	599

Note: 1960 and '66 = 100. Dual base years used; refer to Chapter 3.

Table A-7
Police Department: Crime Investigation—Misdemeanors by Borough

| Year | Citywide | Borough | | | | |
		Manhattan	Bronx	Brooklyn	Queens	Staten Island
1973	109	*85*	116	109	133	173
1972	108	91	114	109	123	169
1971	133	117	139	136	141	**206**
1970	**139**	128	**144**	139	**145**	203
1969	138	**130**	139	**141**	137	197
1968	136	127	142	141	133	168
1967	112	107	116	115	112	115
1966	*100*	100	*100*	*100*	*100*	*100*
Base (1966)	364,091	115,729	57,566	115,201	65,094	10,501
1965	**132**	**166**	**165**	137	**145**	**146**
1964	129	120	147	127	136	136
1963	120	112	137	121	124	118
1962	111	105	119	110	122	110
1961	103	*99*	110	102	108	100
1960	*100*	100	*100*	*100*	*100*	*100*
Base (1960)	227,588	84,328	28,441	71,735	36,415	6,669

Note: 1960 and '66 = 100. Dual base years used; refer to Chapter 3.

Table A-8
Police Department: Crime Investigation—Violations by Borough

| Year | Citywide | Borough | | | | |
		Manhattan	Bronx	Brooklyn	Queens	Staten Island
1973	275	302	**191**	214	**321**	**435**
1972	**341**	**424**	163	**215**	308	302
1971	285	356	157	180	218	306
1970	240	287	139	168	214	332
1969	186	211	119	145	185	309
1968	137	142	101	131	148	272
1967	*97*	*99*	85	*93*	107	105
1966	100	100	100	100	*100*	*100*
Base (1966)	71,549	41,860	9,317	12,412	7,322	618
1965	112	101	**123**	136	121	*76*
1964	110	*97*	107	**139**	134	97
1963	119	112	105	128	**155**	**124**
1962	**131**	**131**	110	133	155	98
1961	112	111	*93*	117	127	94
1960	*100*	100	100	*100*	*100*	100
Base (1960)	74,749	42,359	9,071	14,481	8,198	640

Note: 1960 and '66 = 100. Dual base years used; refer to Chapter 3.

Table A-9

Police Department: Arrests and Summonses—Total Felonies by Borough

Year	Citywide	Borough				
		Manhattan	Bronx	Brooklyn	Queens	Staten Island
1973	157	136	207	144	179	186
1972	169	146	216	165	182	168
1971	176	155	214	180	181	154
1970	162	148	194	165	157	131
1969	129	120	145	136	122	113
1968	110	108	113	114	97	105
1967	107	104	110	110	109	102
1966	100	100	100	100	100	100
Base (1966)	58,026	22,834	10,344	17,284	6,650	914
1965	154	148	171	161	138	152
1964	147	144	160	151	136	160
1963	129	125	137	133	118	148
1962	118	119	124	118	109	108
1961	107	109	108	108	101	93
1960	100	100	100	100	100	100
Base (1960)	35,629	14,750	5,417	10,048	4,880	534

Note: 1960 and '66 = 100. Dual base years used; refer to Chapter 3.

Table A-10

Police Department: Arrests and Summonses—Murder and Nonnegligent Manslaughter by Borough

Year	Citywide	Borough				
		Manhattan	Bronx	Brooklyn	Queens	Staten Island
1973	221	201	388	171	184	380
1972	187	161	369	133	165	300
1971	178	147	257	173	171	140
1970	149	133	215	135	144	200
1969	146	151	198	123	127	180
1968	143	134	197	124	159	40
1967	111	111	146	105	79	120
1966	100	100	100	100	100	100
Base (1966)	643	218	108	244	68	5
1965	170	150	313	149	145	550
1964	171	167	231	165	133	150
1963	150	145	171	143	182	150
1962	133	133	158	118	161	300
1961	137	152	182	115	103	250
1960	100	100	100	100	100	100
Base (1960)	387	151	45	156	33	2

Note: 1960 and '66 = 100. Dual base years used; refer to Chapter 3.

Table A-11
Police Department: Arrests and Summonses—Rape by Borough

Year	Citywide	Manhattan	Bronx	Brooklyn	Queens	Staten Island
				Borough		
1973	154	130	181	157	157	190
1972	118	113	135	111	113	179
1971	89	85	82	94	98	95
1970	82	80	85	*80*	83	111
1969	78	75	71	87	77	74
1968	*75*	*73*	*67*	86	*72*	*53*
1967	95	98	80	99	106	105
1966	100	100	100	100	100	100
Base (1966)	1,120	388	248	331	134	19
1965	120	104	158	122	109	113
1964	113	102	146	111	108	94
1963	100	*97*	130	*94*	*86*	94
1962	103	103	101	105	105	*75*
1961	*97*	99	*95*	97	97	88
1960	100	100	100	100	100	100
Base (1960)	1,128	400	186	387	139	16

Note: 1960 and '66 = 100. Dual base years used; refer to Chapter 3.

Table A-12
Police Department: Arrests and Summonses—Assault by Borough

Year	Citywide	Manhattan	Bronx	Brooklyn	Queens	Staten Island
				Borough		
1973	121	91	131	102	115	132
1972	93	80	109	98	91	103
1971	74	65	87	81	66	74
1970	70	63	79	79	57	55
1969	65	*61*	69	76	43	*53*
1968	*63*	61	*63*	*74*	*41*	67
1967	100	92	108	105	98	110
1966	100	100	100	100	100	100
Base (1966)	13,070	4,925	2,431	3,965	1,566	183
1965	139	124	150	155	141	128
1964	133	121	136	144	141	178
1963	115	105	122	124	118	166
1962	108	100	110	117	112	121
1961	106	104	*92*	113	116	*80*
1960	*100*	*100*	100	*100*	*100*	100
Base (1960)	8,980	3,788	1,521	2,395	1,167	109

Note: 1960 and '66 = 100. Dual base years used; refer to Chapter 3.

Table A-13
Police Department: Arrests and Summonses—Robbery by Borough

Year	Citywide	Borough				
		Manhattan	Bronx	Brooklyn	Queens	Staten Island
1973	288	247	339	268	424	357
1972	317	280	385	296	407	376
1971	287	248	339	291	335	317
1970	216	181	269	221	250	257
1969	178	160	195	184	196	235
1968	155	146	160	163	159	239
1967	125	121	120	133	133	161
1966	*100*	*100*	*100*	*100*	*100*	*100*
Base (1966)	6,065	2,561	1,161	1,733	556	54
1965	143	142	178	131	128	159
1964	131	134	155	114	136	100
1963	121	118	131	115	131	165
1962	114	116	121	114	101	97
1961	*100*	*99*	111	*99*	*92*	*91*
1960	100	100	*100*	100	100	100
Base (1960)	3,767	1,651	533	1,168	381	34

Note: 1960 and '66 = 100. Dual base years used; refer to Chapter 3.

Table A-14
Police Department: Arrests and Summonses—Burglary by Borough

Year	Citywide	Borough				
		Manhattan	Bronx	Brooklyn	Queens	Staten Island
1973	181	148	271	152	213	128
1972	173	170	226	153	172	107
1971	172	167	220	163	155	92
1970	144	133	179	142	139	79
1969	126	116	149	124	129	*74*
1968	119	125	118	121	114	87
1967	110	115	112	105	114	95
1966	*100*	*100*	*100*	*100*	*100*	100
Base (1966)	9,215	2,585	1,819	3,442	1,055	314
1965	140	113	186	152	128	158
1964	144	123	183	153	126	186
1963	127	108	165	136	111	133
1962	109	102	127	111	104	102
1961	103	*96*	120	107	*95*	*84*
1960	*100*	100	*100*	*100*	100	100
Base (1960)	6,358	2,204	972	2,090	925	167

Note: 1960 and '66 = 100. Dual base years used; refer to Chapter 3.

Table A-15

Police Department: Arrests and Summonses—Misdemeanors by Borough

Year	Citywide	Borough				
		Manhattan	Bronx	Brooklyn	Queens	Staten Island
1973	*98*	*75*	106	105	122	201
1972	106	90	108	113	118	221
1971	174	145	176	188	188	390
1970	**197**	**173**	**212**	**203**	**202**	389
1969	180	159	190	194	164	**411**
1968	144	132	139	155	140	275
1967	109	101	116	115	102	144
1966	100	100	*100*	*100*	*100*	*100*
Base (1966)	131,891	48,593	23,341	39,279	18,151	2,527
1965	**140**	**133**	**159**	**132**	**159**	**136**
1964	133	127	143	129	150	136
1963	123	110	131	127	136	134
1962	112	103	111	111	136	126
1961	100	*94*	104	*99*	113	114
1960	*100*	100	*100*	100	*100*	*100*
Base (1960)	99,792	37,525	15,046	32,281	12,938	1,982

Note: 1960 and '66 = 100. Dual base years used; refer to Chapter 3.

Table A-16

Police Department: Arrests and Summonses—Violations, Traffic Infractions, and for Other Authorities by Borough

Year[a]	Citywide	Borough				
		Manhattan	Bronx	Brooklyn	Queens	Staten Island
1970	**104**	99	**118**	106	109	110
1969	104	96	117	**108**	**115**	**116**
1968	*88*	*83*	*87*	*88*	104	109
1967	96	97	79	98	110	103
1966	100	**100**	100	100	*100*	*100*
Base (1966)	3,053,541	1,633,757	403,076	578,143	394,313	44,252
1965	**130**	**129**	**139**	**125**	**130**	175
1964	119	117	128	116	124	137
1963	115	118	110	116	108	114
1962	114	117	106	115	108	106
1961	104	104	*96*	106	106	113
1960	*100*	*100*	100	*100*	*100*	*100*
Base (1960)	2,226,810	1,117,405	294,144	477,748	313,304	24,209

Note: 1960 and '66 = 100. Dual base years used; refer to Chapter 3.

[a]The latest year available is 1970.

Table A-17
Police Department: Specialized Units and Services

Year[a]	Traffic Safety	Emergency Services	Bomb Squad Cases Investigated	Missing Persons Unit Persons Reported Missing	Unidentified Dead, Sick, etc.	Searches for Missing from Other Locations
1970	129	**176**	**1,035**	144	50	**244**
1969	**132**	136	320	**147**	70	129
1968	132	129	165	134	78	120
1967	123	160	128	136	105	116
1966	121	141	110	123	**106**	96
1965	113	126	102	114	99	105
1964	113	100	104	115	95	95
1963	106	105	90	109	97	143
1962	103	110	87	106	100	155
1961	95	99	72	100	98	133
1960	100	100	100	100	100	100
Base	37,472	27,872	996	9,555	20,386	2,287

Note: 1960 = 100.

[a]The latest year available is 1970.

Table A-18
Police Department: Specialized Units—Harbor Precinct

Year[a]	Searches	Rescues	Cooperation and Special Assignments	Accidents, etc.
1970	652	**342**	153	193
1969	**712**	187	100	124
1968	542	258	140	**222**
1967	452	335	**282**	152
1966	302	300	153	213
1965	233	248	285	148
1964	175	213	125	143
1963	112	207	106	128
1962	171	203	82	150
1961	*90*	161	*76*	117
1960	100	*100*	100	*100*
Base	89	31	201	46

Note: 1960 = 100.

[a]The latest year available is 1970.

Table A-19
Police Department: Specialized Units—Aviation Unit

Year[a]	Aerial Traffic Survey	Searches	Escorts, etc.
1970	133	281	404
1969	156	295	557
1968	152	**530**	677
1967	177	310	**1,242**
1966	**364**	134	366
1965	183	172	337
1964	145	*43*	158
1963	185	43	529
1962	193	88	78
1961	167	55	*49*
1960	*100*	100	100
Base	287	88	113

Note: 1960 = 100.

[a]The latest year available is 1970.

Table A-20
Police Department: Supportive Services

Year[a]	Police Lab		ID Section	Ballistics	Photo Section		Licensing	Property Clerk		Medical Unit	
	Criminal Investigations	Narcotics as a Percent of Total	Finger-prints	Cases	Assignments	Prisoners Photo-graphed	Licenses Processed, etc.	Lots of Property Received	Autos Received	Examina-tions	X-Rays
1970	484	93	118	279	167	287	123	1,519	473	213	185
1969	355	91	120	241	174	233	126	197	463	314	150
1968	238	85	103	264	169	189	108	174	425	275	129
1967	216	80	93	194	179	177	106	161	390	253	120
1966	182	78	106	159	158	166	99	147	100	253	112
1965	146	73	122	139	136	165	101	136	b	154	100
1964	134	72	111	121	132	165	91	135		176	c
1963	108	66	113	113	127	142	110	118		185	
1962	101	62	107	113	110	130	108	111		148	
1961	90	60	90	108	104	126	95	99		123	
1960	100	63	100	100	100	100	100	100		100	
Base	10,527	6,657	266,142	3,353	3,524	47,527	110,778	58,236	23,415	3,019	20,234

[a] The latest year available is 1970.

[b] Auto tow-away program began in 1966 (1966 = 100).

[c] The first year data are available is 1965 (1965 = 100).

Table A-21
Police Department: Clearance Rates—Total Felonies by Borough

Year	Citywide	Borough				
		Manhattan	Bronx	Brooklyn	Queens	Staten Island
1973	19.3	18.9	25.0	*17.4*	17.7	*11.7*
1972	22.5	20.7	31.6	21.3	*15.4*	12.3
1971	22.2	21.2	23.2	22.9	22.5	15.1
1970	23.6	22.9	25.4	26.5	19.3	13.1
1969	24.2	23.1	27.6	27.6	17.5	14.8
1968	22.1	20.6	23.5	25.2	18.2	17.9
1967	19.4	16.4	23.6	22.3	17.4	16.7
1966	*17.9*	*16.7*	*17.9*	19.8	17.4	16.8
1965	34.5	32.4	37.3	35.0	37.2	31.3
1964	33.9	33.5	37.4	33.9	32.4	28.7
1963	34.9	32.4	**40.3**	36.0	35.1	36.1
1962	**35.5**	**34.6**	38.6	34.4	37.2	34.9
1961	35.4	32.5	39.9	**36.3**	**39.1**	28.8
1960	34.5	32.2	38.3	35.1	37.2	**36.9**

Note: These are the actual clearance rates computed as the ratio ot cases cleared to net cases.

Table A-22
Police Department: Clearance Rates by Type of Crime

Year	Murder	Rape	Assault	Robbery	Burglary	Misdemeanors	Violations
1973	69	37	50	19	14	42	94
1972	57	*31*	41	19	19	42	96
1971	57	31	*39*	25	16	49	95
1970	68	37	42	24	18	**50**	94
1969	65	36	41	28	20	48	92
1968	76	42	40	25	18	*41*	*91*
1967	78	51	47	20	14	41	**99**
1966	75	54	46	*18*	*11*	41	99
1965	83	73	66	43	**29**	49	99
1964	88	75	68	43	28	50	99
1963	**89**	78	68	**44**	29	50	99
1962	89	77	67	44	29	50	99
1961	87	**80**	68	42	28	49	99
1960	89	78	70	42	28	50	99

Note: These are actual clearance rates computed as the ratio of cases cleared to net cases.

Table A-23
Police Department: Property Recovery Rates

Year	Motor Vehicles	Other Property
1973	32.0	5.0
1972	*26.5*	5.3
1971	n.a.	n.a.
1970	44.1	4.8
1969	45.9	**8.2**
1968	54.8	4.2
1967	56.8	*3.6*
1966	54.9	5.0
1965	71.3	3.7
1964	76.6	3.6
1963	83.0	3.9
1962	86.2	3.5
1961	89.7	5.6
1960	**90.4**	5.0

Note: These are actual recovery rates; n.a. = not available.

Table A-24
Fire Department: Fires Extinguished—Total by Borough

Year	Citywide	Manhattan	Bronx	Brooklyn	Queens	Staten Island
		\multicolumn{5}{Borough}				
1972	194	169	241	207	154	**192**
1971	206	**187**	247	223	159	191
1970	209	179	250	**242**	158	173
1969	207	179	253	231	**162**	176
1968	**210**	179	**263**	235	159	176
1967	150	138	170	171	120	102
1966	148	132	164	160	131	155
1965	140	124	151	153	129	143
1964	130	121	141	138	123	115
1963	123	115	119	129	125	126
1962	115	109	111	120	115	127
1961	101	106	*96*	103	*98*	*98*
1960	*100*	*100*	100	*100*	100	100
Base	60,941	15,292	12,687	18,575	11,026	3,361

Note: 1960 = 100.

Table A-25
Fire Department: Fires Extinguished—Residential by Borough

Year	Citywide	Borough				
		Manhattan	Bronx	Brooklyn	Queens	Staten Island
1972	206	152	300	186	177	275
1971	180	153	226	219	169	324
1970	174	145	223	180	163	249
1969	173	144	222	180	168	210
1968	171	146	213	179	162	192
1967	156	136	186	165	146	166
1966	141	125	162	148	134	150
1965	134	124	148	138	130	135
1964	127	119	132	135	124	121
1963	117	114	117	119	120	122
1962	110	109	107	113	107	116
1961	102	103	100	101	102	110
1960	*100*	*100*	*100*	*100*	*100*	*100*
Base	18,585	6,777	3,481	5,601	2,452	274

Note: 1960 = 100.

Table A-26
Fire Department: Fires Extinguished—Commercial by Borough

Year	Citywide	Borough				
		Manhattan	Bronx	Brooklyn	Queens	Staten Island
1972	134	106	157	157	133	166
1971	119	107	129	124	126	141
1970	117	103	121	130	116	148
1969	122	108	128	128	133	132
1968	123	107	132	131	135	131
1967	108	99	115	109	122	111
1966	112	107	116	112	123	103
1965	116	107	128	119	122	114
1964	108	102	125	108	110	95
1963	115	108	118	117	125	110
1962	113	106	120	114	119	115
1961	106	102	103	110	114	*90*
1960	*100*	100	*100*	*100*	*100*	100
Base	5,501	1,990	770	1,640	955	140

Note: 1960 = 100.

144

Table A-27
Fire Department: Fires Extinguished—Public Places by Borough

Year	Citywide	Borough				
		Manhattan	Bronx	Brooklyn	Queens	Staten Island
1972	212	254	269	344	207	267
1971	236	231	253	285	174	191
1970	247	253	210	302	201	215
1969	253	246	272	307	185	206
1968	215	225	212	261	150	155
1967	190	200	182	230	137	142
1966	149	169	146	152	125	91
1965	133	151	105	145	124	67
1964	137	156	117	153	109	97
1963	125	146	116	134	89	79
1962	115	123	102	128	103	67
1961	90	94	70	98	90	79
1960	100	100	100	100	100	100
Base	785	265	130	207	150	33

Note: 1960 = 100.

Table A-28
Fire Department: Fires Extinguished—Vacant Buildings by Borough

Year	Citywide	Borough				
		Manhattan	Bronx	Brooklyn	Queens	Staten Island
1972	231	124	317	384	122	290
1971	256	170	288	305	101	196
1970	257	150	296	394	115	161
1969	240	138	290	349	126	200
1968	232	144	231	371	107	183
1967	139	77	118	237	75	158
1966	122	73	57	227	92	132
1965	100	60	44	182	78	169
1964	82	62	43	126	73	161
1963	74	67	39	102	72	127
1962	81	72	49	117	66	135
1961	89	114	58	95	71	128
1960	100	100	100	100	100	100
Base	2,736	759	650	861	395	71

Note: 1960 = 100.

Table A-29
Fire Department: Fires Extinguished—Miscellaneous by Borough

Year	Citywide	Borough				
		Manhattan	Bronx	Brooklyn	Queens	Staten Island
1972	212	233	243	223	156	184
1971	229	259	265	244	163	185
1970	239	249	272	279	164	167
1969	236	252	277	263	166	174
1968	244	247	303	270	165	177
1967	153	160	173	179	113	94
1966	160	155	179	169	133	159
1965	152	138	165	164	132	145
1964	140	138	155	146	140	114
1963	131	123	127	134	130	128
1962	121	114	118	125	120	129
1961	101	112	96	105	96	97
1960	100	100	100	100	100	100
Base	33,334	5,501	7,656	10,266	7,074	2,837

Note: 1960 = 100.

Table A-30
Fire Department: Response to False Alarms by Borough

Year	Citywide	Borough				
		Manhattan	Bronx	Brooklyn	Queens	Staten Island
1972	655	435	980	665	584	558
1971	643	431	902	702	551	482
1970	542	331	725	659	430	322
1969	441	281	601	506	380	293
1968	373	238	514	428	314	244
1967	295	186	323	377	268	169
1966	229	156	255	284	206	144
1965	201	147	211	240	198	118
1964	164	131	173	183	169	106
1963	135	119	139	146	135	87
1962	124	112	126	132	128	98
1961	113	114	119	116	106	91
1960	100	100	100	100	100	100
Base	16,326	3,799	3,206	5,710	3,098	513

Note: 1960 = 100.

Table A-31

Fire Department: Response to Emergencies by Borough, Multiple Alarm Fires

Year	Citywide	Borough					Multiple-alarm Fires
		Manhattan	Bronx	Brooklyn	Queens	Staten Island	
1972	**294**	265	**428**	277	253	**436**	180
1971	294	**271**	413	**280**	**256**	360	190
1970	273	248	401	263	229	306	193
1969	243	229	342	230	211	283	205
1968	233	225	326	217	202	240	**218**
1967	197	196	262	184	170	215	156
1966	161	165	206	147	142	180	147
1965	144	147	179	135	128	142	148
1964	131	134	157	125	120	127	121
1963	124	130	134	116	118	118	159
1962	111	115	114	110	104	110	152
1961	104	110	105	103	*96*	*93*	112
1960	*100*	*100*	*100*	*100*	100	100	*100*
Base	16,868	5,102	2,403	5,940	3,034	389	287

Note: 1960 = 100.

Table A-32

Fire Department: Fire-prevention Activities

Year	Buildings Inspected	Permits Issued	School[a] Lectures	General[a] Lectures	Violation Orders & Summonses Issued
1972	*76*	77	7	*33*	*47*
1971	89	85	*6*	101	60
1970	101	103	11	127	68
1969	105	104	12	67	70
1968	121	97	7	**179**	78
1967	160	81	256	70	139
1966	164	101	257	41	156
1965	177	**121**	247	14	207
1964	**185**	93	260	19	**335**
1963	116	108	313	39	121
1962	109	104	**323**	59	185
1961	111	106	100	100	99
1960	100	100	—	—	100
Base	866,429	265,841	5,861	950	179,151

Note: 1960 = 100.

[a]1961 = 100.

Table A-33
Fire Department: Medical and Investigative Activities

	Medical			Investigative	
Year	Personnel Examinations	Member Visits	Doctor Response to Fires	Arrests	Investigations[a]
1972	22	240	413	261	32
1971	36	227	280	227	53
1970	72	210	234	285	171
1969	72	180	164	335	170
1968	27	155	154	252	167
1967	45	139	128	244	144
1966	65	130	144	203	132
1965	61	124	155	188	126
1964	47	131	145	159	118
1963	72	133	143	137	111
1962	68	115	161	132	107
1961	48	98	110	101	100
1960	100	100	100	100	–
Base	5,323	16,021	642	186	27,874

Note: 1960 = 100.
[a]1961 = 100.

Table A-34
Social Services: Total Public-assistance Cases by Borough

		Borough				
Year[a]	Citywide	Manhattan	Bronx	Brooklyn	Queens	Staten Island
1973	378	226	392	438	1,208	455
1972	372	238	369	425	1,186	428
1971	336	217	330	395	1,040	369
1970	291	189	283	346	870	300
1969	272	185	242	324	807	237
1968	217	148	253	261	374	178
1967	167	117	179	186	294	142
1960	100	100	100	100	100	100
Base	135,318	49,620	24,253	42,412	7,139	1,409

Note: 1960 = 100.
[a]Selected years.

Table A-35
Social Services: AFDC Cases by Borough

Year[a]	Citywide	Borough				
		Manhattan	Bronx	Brooklyn	Queens	Staten Island
1973	522	247	613	617	2,011	659
1972	514	257	584	602	2,007	624
1971	486	249	538	577	1,839	561
1970	420	218	460	505	1,546	451
1969	396	212	389	479	1,500	378
1968	310	164	408	380	624	280
1967	236	130	280	268	492	212
1960	100	100	100	100	100	100
Base	48,344	16,908	8,761	16,900	2,200	47

Note: 1960 = 100.

[a]Selected years.

Table A-36
Social Services: Average Monthly Number of Cases

Year[a]	Total	AFDC	Home Relief	Old-age Assistance	Aid to the Disabled	Blind Assistance
1973	368	522	344	171	448	114
1972	381	531	402	180	444	113
1971	351	507	381	179	342	105
1970	308	456	381	161	239	99
1969	280	416	411	140	179	95
1968	241	352	413	122	114	87
1967	189	274	288	107	100	85
1966	153	213	202	90	88	82
1965	141	181	174	78	87	82
1964	127	157	140	76	89	82
1963	114	135	105	75	89	83
1962	108	120	89	76	92	84
1961	103	114	96	83	98	89
1960	100	100	100	100	100	100
Base	135,376	47,497	18,714	41,939	24,722	2,504

Note: 1960 = 100.

[a]An average for the 12 months in the year.

Table A-37
Social Services: Average Monthly Number of Applications Received

Year[a]	Total	AFDC	Home Relief	Old-age Assistance	Aid to the Disabled	Blind Assistance
1973	155	171	121	93	303	77
1972	187	164	168	121	412	89
1971	188	175	148	137	439	89
1970	186	209	140	161	324	98
1969	163	172	142	158	224	86
1968	184	202	198	136	129	105
1967	158	185	157	137	98	100
1966	134	157	119	116	100	105
1965	145	140	106	71	86	91
1964	147	142	102	76	96	102
1963	142	144	89	75	100	100
1962	132	128	78	76	99	102
1961	118	117	91	88	98	91
1960	100	100	100	100	100	100
Base	11,344	3,909	4,785	1,364	1,242	44

Note: 1960 = 100.

[a]An average for the 12 months in the year.

Table A-38
Social Services: Care Facilities

Year[a]	Adult-shelter Care		Child Welfare— Persons Under Care	Dental-care Procedures[b]	Optical Care Procedures[b]
	Average Daily Census	Meals Provided			
1973	57	62	n.a.	48	n.a.
1972	62	63	n.a.	44	n.a.
1971	61	61	237	41	n.a.
1970	60	57	217	46	n.a.
1969	58	54	204	46	n.a.
1968	65	64	186	62	n.a.
1967	68	65	138	138	186
1966	79	77	129	120	90
1965	84	81	118	151	134
1964	79	84	114	144	149
1963	89	94	111	132	129
1962	87	97	114	125	120
1961	101	107	102	116	98
1960	100	100	100	100	100
Base	3,790	315,378	19,847	31,225	2,594

Note: 1960 = 100; n.a. = not available.

[a]As of January of each year.

[b]A procedure can range from a simple examination to complex surgical work.

Table A-39
Social Services: Cases Closed

Year[a]	Total	AFDC	Home Relief	Old-age Assistance	Aid to the Disabled	Blind Assistance
1973	**312**	384	324	140	304	75
1972	281	211	326	**157**	**433**	68
1971	208	185	229	121	262	63
1970	198	187	222	128	233	65
1969	243	212	**379**	134	146	51
1968	142	142	191	98	92	66
1967	132	132	165	107	96	79
1966	125	126	126	78	85	57
1965	*47*	*36*	*27*	*39*	*26*	*31*
1964	147	118	98	89	89	74
1963	149	114	83	98	95	76
1962	148	109	84	93	99	74
1961	92	83	98	93	97	79
1960	100	100	100	100	100	**100**
Base	6,821	2,290	2,267	951	1,245	68

Note: 1960 = 100.

[a]An average for the 12 months in the year.

Table A-40
Social Services: Cases Closed Due to Employment

Year[a]	Total	AFDC	Home Relief	Old-age Assistance	Aid to the Disabled	Blind Assistance
1973	66	59	74	*16*	74	43
1972	96	83	110	46	114	14
1971	93	108	80	46	91	29
1970	92	99	81	54	**133**	43
1969	139	146	147	41	83	43
1968	**162**	188	**159**	57	57	*0*
1967	113	147	90	76	53	57
1966	110	150	82	46	50	71
1965	*31*	*44*	*20*	24	*13*	57
1964	102	141	71	57	69	57
1963	90	129	59	54	60	29
1962	96	132	65	78	70	71
1961	87	76	101	70	86	43
1960	100	100	100	**100**	100	**100**
Base	1,563	711	699	37	109	7

Note: 1960 = 100.

[a]An average for the 12 months in the year.

Table A-41
Social Services: Cases Closed Due to Ineligibility

Year[a]	Total	AFDC	Aid to the Disabled	Blind Assistance
1973	**274**	**272**	277	300
1972	179	216	92	b
1971	135	179	25	b
1970	160	197	69	b
1969	125	161	37	b
1968	117	143	55	b
1967	87	105	42	100
1966	70	72	64	100
1965	*11*	*13*	*6*	b
1964	72	77	58	b
1963	65	65	64	100
1962	70	63	88	100
1961	84	93	62	b
1960	100	100	100	100
Base	367	261	106	1

Note: 1960 = 100.

[a]An average for the 12 months in the year.

[b]Zero or less than 1.

Table A-42
Health and Hospital: Average Daily Census

Year	All Inpatients	General Care	Psychiatric Care	Tubercular Care	Newborn Nursery	Chronic & Extended Care	Drug Addiction[a]
1973	78	90	78	33	77	70	319
1972	81	78	77	44	76	75	391
1971	85	96	82	57	88	77	358
1970	87	97	89	59	98	83	70
1969	89	95	95	67	88	90	70
1968	92	97	91	88	83	95	100
1967	96	98	95	105	95	99	100
1966	100	100	100	100	100	100	–
Base	13,956	7,191	1,350	1,216	456	3,272	43

Note: 1966 = 100.
[a]1967 = 100.

Table A-43
Health and Hospital: Admissions

Year	All Inpatient	General Care	Psychiatric	Tubercular	Newborn	Chronic & Extended Care	Drug Addiction[a]
1973	98	105	73	63	66	108	263
1972	100	107	74	68	68	76	357
1971	104	111	75	70	78	71	471
1970	99	103	85	66	87	75	50
1969	92	94	86	85	77	79	47
1968	95	96	93	95	77	94	77
1967	99	97	99	94	91	92	100
1966	100	100	100	100	100	100	—
Base	253,680	207,840	34,885	3,961	36,577	3,811	880

Note: 1966 = 100.

[a] 1967 = 100.

Table A-44
Health and Hospital: Ambulatory-care Visits and Laboratory Tests

Year	Ambulatory Care		Laboratory Tests	
	Emergency Room	Outpatient	Inpatient	Outpatient
1973	**113**	**141**	**198**	**343**
1972	111	121	184	262
1971	108	93	179	246
1970	105	87	154	166
1969	96	*82*	133	128
1968	*92*	84	124	115
1967	98	91	115	106
1966	100	100	*100*	*100*
Base ('000)	1,507	3,398	9,973	2,830

Note: 1966 = 100.

Table A-45
Health and Hospital: Average Length of Stay by Type of Care

Year	General	Psychiatric	Tubercular	Newborn	Chronic	Drug Addiction[a]
1973	85	107	52	100	63	117
1972	85	107	62	100	94	106
1971	85	107	81	100	103	78
1970	92	107	78	100	106	133
1969	100	114	66	100	101	144
1968	100	100	79	100	100	128
1967	100	100	95	100	104	100
1966	100	100	100	100	100	–
Base (days)	13	14	111	5	313	18

Note: The lower the index, the greater the performance. 1966 = 100.

a1967 = 100.

Table A-46
Department of Sanitation: Refuse Collection—Tons Collected by Borough

| Year | Citywide | Borough | | | | |
		Manhattan	Bronx	Brooklyn	Queens	Staten Island
1972-73	141	118	162	136	148	193
1971-72	143	124	165	133	150	186
1970-71	137	124	162	128	140	171
1969-70	132	121	152	123	138	159
1968-69	125	116	146	117	129	142
1967-68	121	112	135	115	126	139
1966-67	118	112	135	111	120	132
1965-66	114	110	131	106	115	128
1964-65	111	109	119	105	113	126
1963-64	106	104	113	102	107	126
1962-63	100	102	106	95	100	109
1961-62	102	104	106	98	103	108
1960-61	100	100	100	100	100	100
Base	2,758,210	600,819	439,174	920,766	692,674	104,777

Note: 1960-61 = 100.

Table A-47
Department of Sanitation: Street Cleaning—Miles Swept by Borough

| Year | Citywide | Borough | | | | |
		Manhattan	Bronx	Brooklyn	Queens	Staten Island
1972-73	178	161	181	210	168	94
1971-72	152	149	153	171	143	75
1970-71	152	148	164	159	146	108
1969-70	116	130	135	120	88	39
1968-69	118	141	139	126	75	15
1967-68	123	137	128	135	96	37
1966-67	112	120	118	119	95	63
1965-66	125	127	128	132	120	83
1964-65	123	128	126	123	123	95
1963-64	120	123	125	121	114	100
1962-63	119	123	124	113	123	102
1961-62	113	119	118	104	115	121
1960-61	100	100	100	100	100	100
Base	740,001	229,739	97,801	245,475	130,764	36,222

Note: 1960-61 = 100.

Table A-48
Department of Sanitation: Street Cleaning—Miles Flushed by Borough

Year	Citywide	Borough				
		Manhattan	Bronx	Brooklyn	Queens	Staten Island
1972-73	63	43	87	93	81	73
1971-72	43	31	50	63	55	41
1970-71	50	27	85	68	73	96
1969-70	21	*21*	40	23	12	13
1968-69	*19*	25	23	*16*	2	5
1967-68	36	51	27	30	18	*4*
1966-67	49	54	26	47	52	24
1965-66	27	30	*15*	25	31	8
1964-65	64	72	47	42	76	51
1963-64	69	73	73	52	76	44
1962-63	89	92	99	62	**102**	95
1961-62	95	96	**113**	75	98	**110**
1960-61	**100**	**100**	100	**100**	100	100
Base	430,200	228,757	41,638	77,225	68,646	13,934

Note: 1960-61 = 100.

Table A-49
Department of Sanitation: Street Cleaning—Manual Cleaning Man-Days by Borough

Year	Citywide	Borough				
		Manhattan	Bronx	Brooklyn	Queens	Staten Island
1972-73	69	79	*80*	13	39	*78*
1971-72	*52*	84	98	88	*34*	115
1970-71	86	72	**122**	**103**	69	161
1969-70	56	*47*	91	*62*	48	99
1968-69	65	54	98	75	57	116
1967-68	71	72	93	67	59	160
1966-67	81	89	86	67	74	**194**
1965-66	92	98	90	81	92	165
1964-65	88	88	88	85	90	118
1963-64	90	90	89	88	89	124
1962-63	90	88	95	89	93	93
1961-62	**104**	97	117	103	**113**	104
1960-61	100	**100**	100	100	100	100
Base	154,577	61,950	11,977	46,461	31,859	2,330

Note: 1960-61 = 100.

Table A-50
Department of Sanitation: Snow and Ice Removal—Miles Plowed per Inch Fall by Borough

Year	Citywide	Borough				
		Manhattan	Bronx	Brooklyn	Queens	Staten Island
1972-73	3	17	4	6	a	3
1971-72	38	33	66	59	26	31
1970-71	70	91	130	107	47	42
1969-70	74	122	105	103	51	65
1968-69	85	142	95	127	62	65
1967-68	5	2	3	8	4	4
1966-67	55	68	63	43	55	55
1965-66	45	63	65	44	41	30
1964-65	67	92	46	62	73	46
1963-64	43	46	28	37	5	47
1962-63	12	42	4	8	10	11
1961-62	10	23	19	7	6	16
1960-61	100	100	100	100	100	100
Base	3,485	301	372	641	1,791	380

Note: 1960-61 = 100.
aZero or less than 1.

Table A-51
Department of Sanitation: Snow and Ice Removal—Miles Salt Spread per Inch Fall by Borough

Year	Citywide	Borough				
		Manhattan	Bronx	Brooklyn	Queens	Staten Island
1972-73	568	478	644	548	598	563
1971-72	306	211	279	370	320	370
1970-71	476	414	451	520	460	644
1969-70	353	252	386	432	330	426
1968-69	264	214	265	281	280	269
1967-68	280	260	221	324	300	234
1966-67	176	204	137	149	202	139
1965-66	239	287	211	243	244	130
1964-65	245	304	198	181	289	171
1963-64	135	153	123	98	97	111
1962-63	309	342	296	251	327	334
1961-62	225	259	264	192	206	227
1960-61	100	100	100	100	100	100
Base	1,439	297	234	321	483	105

Note: 1960-61 = 100.

Table A-52

Department of Sanitation: Towing Operations—Vehicles Towed by Borough

Year	Citywide	Borough				
		Manhattan	Bronx	Brooklyn	Queens	Staten Island
1972-73	5	3	a	11	a	39
1971-72	*3*	2	a	8	a	a
1970-71	28	108	a	5	1	a
1969-70	33	128	a	*3*	1	6
1968-69	73	**270**	a	11	1	150
1967-68	117	205	19	**157**	65	124
1966-67	117	147	79	145	81	158
1965-66	**136**	148	**141**	148	88	**231**
1964-65	122	122	126	133	**100**	120
1963-64	100	100	100	100	100	100
Base	14,865	3,671	3,689	4,423	2,840	242

Note: 1963-64 = 100.

aZero or less than 1.

Table A-53

Department of Sanitation: Towing Operations—Towing Truck Shifts by Borough

Year	Citywide	Borough				
		Manhattan	Bronx	Brooklyn	Queens	Staten Island
1972-73	51	30	41	102	a	65
1971-72	*43*	*27*	55	79	a	a
1970-71	50	115	64	34	3	3
1969-70	41	114	72	*6*	1	3
1968-69	68	**238**	*23*	11	2	289
1967-68	128	187	125	129	66	160
1966-67	125	126	**141**	143	85	121
1965-66	**135**	136	140	**153**	91	352
1964-65	123	127	124	137	98	128
1963-64	100	100	100	100	**100**	100
Base	6,098	1,456	940	2,203	1,433	66

Note: 1963-64 = 100.

aZero or less than 1.

Table A-54
Department of Sanitation: Refuse Disposal by Borough

Year	Total Tons Handled	Incineration	Truck Landfill	Marine Transfer
1972-73	155	*81*	223	146
1971-72	149	89	200	147
1970-71	135	102	152	145
1969-70	124	102	117	153
1968-69	121	113	111	141
1967-68	126	132	110	139
1966-67	117	136	99	122
1965-66	112	130	94	116
1964-65	106	125	85	111
1963-64	105	126	*65*	110
1962-63	108	130	88	111
1961-62	106	116	104	*98*
1960-61	*100*	100	100	100
Base ('000)	5,877	1,717	2,168	1,974

Note: 1960-61 = 100.

Table A-55
Department of Sanitation: Refuse Collection—Tons per Man-Day by Borough

Year	Citywide	Borough				
		Manhattan	Bronx	Brooklyn	Queens	Staten Island
1972-73	126	111	143	112	142	147
1971-72	122	121	141	106	137	142
1970-71	113	116	136	98	122	133
1969-70	109	116	127	99	112	128
1968-69	101	113	127	95	116	122
1967-68	108	108	132	96	114	112
1966-67	108	110	124	99	112	110
1965-66	105	108	125	95	108	108
1964-65	103	107	115	95	106	109
1963-64	100	104	111	94	103	110
1962-63	*96*	103	102	*90*	*97*	*100*
1961-62	97	104	*97*	93	99	100
1960-61	100	*100*	100	100	100	100
Base	2.64	2.88	2.66	2.84	2.22	2.24

Note: 1960-61 = 100.

Table A-56

Department of Sanitation: Street Cleaning—Miles Swept per Miles in Area by Borough

Year	Citywide	Borough				
		Manhattan	Bronx	Brooklyn	Queens	Staten Island
1972-73	146	157	187	186	107	91
1971-72	125	145	158	152	92	72
1970-71	125	144	170	142	94	105
1969-70	95	127	139	107	56	39
1968-69	102	145	157	118	51	14
1967-68	106	140	145	126	65	36
1966-67	112	120	118	117	95	64
1965-66	125	127	128	129	121	83
1964-65	122	128	125	120	123	94
1963-64	119	123	125	118	114	100
1962-63	118	123	124	110	123	103
1961-62	112	119	117	101	115	121
1960-61	100	100	100	100	100	100
Base	77.6	201.4	65.0	87.0	43.0	36.0

Note: 1960-61 = 100.

Table A-57

Department of Sanitation: Street Cleaning—Miles Flushed per Miles in Area by Borough

Year	Citywide	Borough				
		Manhattan	Bronx	Brooklyn	Queens	Staten Island
1972-73	52	42	91	82	51	71
1971-72	35	30	52	56	35	40
1970-71	41	27	88	60	47	93
1969-70	18	20	41	21	6	12
1968-69	16	26	27	15	1	4
1967-68	31	53	31	28	12	4
1966-67	48	54	26	46	52	24
1965-66	27	30	15	24	31	8
1964-65	64	72	47	42	75	51
1963-64	68	73	73	51	76	44
1962-63	88	92	99	61	102	95
1961-62	94	96	113	74	98	110
1960-61	100	100	100	100	100	100
Base	45.10	200.54	27.53	27.30	22.60	13.82

Note: 1960-61 = 100.

Table A-58

Department of Sanitation: Snow and Ice Removal—Miles Plowed per Miles in Area by Borough

Year	Citywide	Borough				
		Manhattan	Bronx	Brooklyn	Queens	Staten Island
1972-73	a	*1*	a	a	a	a
1971-72	13	13	29	22	7	13
1970-71	15	23	35	25	8	11
1969-70	27	54	49	41	15	28
1968-69	39	77	57	63	22	33
1967-68	1	1	1	3	1	2
1966-67	49	61	56	38	33	49
1965-66	17	23	24	16	15	11
1964-65	28	39	20	26	31	20
1963-64	34	36	22	28	37	37
1962-63	3	12	1	2	3	3
1961-62	3	7	6	2	2	5
1960-61	**100**	**100**	**100**	**100**	**100**	**100**
Base	20.99	15.11	14.10	13.00	33.71	21.62

Note: 1960-61 = 100.
aZero or less than 1.

Table A-59

Department of Sanitation: Snow and Ice Removal—Miles Salted per Curb Miles in Area by Borough

Year	Citywide	Borough				
		Manhattan	Bronx	Brooklyn	Queens	Staten Island
1972-73	*25*	*24*	*35*	*24*	*20*	*29*
1971-72	107	87	122	139	86	152
1970-71	100	103	119	120	75	160
1969-70	130	110	**179**	**172**	95	**185**
1968-69	121	116	158	139	99	140
1967-68	82	90	84	102	68	78
1966-67	**158**	**183**	123	131	**181**	126
1965-66	90	107	79	89	91	49
1964-65	105	129	84	75	123	73
1963-64	105	119	96	75	124	88
1962-63	88	97	84	70	93	96
1961-62	71	82	83	60	65	72
1960-61	100	100	100	100	100	100
Base	8.60	14.93	8.90	6.50	9.10	5.94

Note: 1960-61 = 100.

Table A-60

Department of Sanitation: Towing Operations—Vehicles Towed per Truck Shift by Borough

| Year | Citywide | Borough | | | | |
		Manhattan	Bronx	Brooklyn	Queens	Staten Island
1972-73	9	10	a	11	a	60
1971-72	7	6	a	10	a	a
1970-71	56	94	a	15	29	a
1969-70	79	112	a	55	77	203
1968-69	107	115	a	106	68	51
1967-68	91	111	15	121	100	77
1966-67	94	119	56	101	95	130
1965-66	103	108	102	97	96	65
1964-65	99	96	102	100	101	92
1963-64	100	100	100	100	100	100
Base	2.44	2.52	3.92	2.01	2.00	3.70

Note: 1963-64 = 100.

aZero or less than 1.

Table A-61

Department of Sanitation: Refuse Disposal—Tons per Man-Day

Year	Incinerator	Truck Landfill	Marine Transfer
1972-73	115	214	142
1971-72	116	194	143
1970-71	120	195	139
1969-70	115	134	140
1968-69	111	147	138
1967-68	117	137	133
1966-67	114	127	105
1965-66	110	122	115
1964-65	105	106	110
1963-64	106	104	106
1962-63	110	115	107
1961-62	101	107	92
1960-61	100	100	100
Base	8.51	44.25	65.92

Note: 1960-61 = 100.

Bibliography

Bibliography

Published Material

Abascal, Ralph S. "Municipal Services and Equal Protection: Variations on a Theme by Griffen v. Illinois." *Hastings Law Journal* 20 (May 1969): 1367-91.

Allison, John P. "Economic Factors and the Rate of Crime." *Land Economics* 48 (May 1972): 193-96.

American Federalism: Toward a More Effective Partnership. The National Conference of American Federalism in Action. Washington, D.C.: February 20-22, 1975.

Anderson, Dennis R. "Toward the Equalization of Municipal Services: Variations on a Theme by Hawkins." *Journal of Urban Law* 50 (November 1972): 177-97.

Bahl, Roy W. "Public Policy and the Urban Fiscal Problem: Piecemeal vs. Aggregate Solutions." *Land Economics* 46 (February 1970): 41-50.

————. "Studies on Determinants of Public Expenditures: A Review." *Functional Federalism: Grants-in-Aid and PPB Systems.* Selma J. Mushkin and John F. Cotton, eds. Washington, D.C.: State Local Finances Project of The George Washington University, 1968: 184-207.

Bahl, Roy W., Alan K. Campbell, and David Greytak. *Taxes, Expenditures, and the Economic Base: Case Study of New York City.* New York: Praeger Publishers, 1974.

Baumol, William J. "Macroeconomics of Unbalanced Growth: The Anatomy of Urban Crisis." *American Economic Review* 57 (June 1967): 415-26.

————. "Macroeconomics of Unbalanced Growth: Comment." *American Economic Review* 58 (September 1968): 896-97.

Bell, Carolyn Shaw. "Macroeconomics of Unbalanced Growth: Comment." *American Economic Review* 58 (September 1968): 877-84.

Bish, Robert L. *The Public Economy of Metropolitan Areas.* Chicago: Markham, 1971.

Bish, Robert L., and Hugh O. Nourse. *Urban Economics and Policy Analysis.* New York: McGraw-Hill, 1975.

Bish, Robert L., and Vincent Ostrom. *Understanding Urban Government: Metropolitan Reform Reconsidered.* Washington, D.C.: American Enterprise Institute for Public Policy Research, 1973.

Blum, Edward H. *Urban Fire Protection: Studies of the Operations of the New York Fire Department.* New York: New York City RAND Institute, 1971.

Braford, D.S., R.A. Malt, and W.E. Oates. "The Rising Cost of Local Public Services: Some Evidence and Reflections." *National Tax Journal* 22 (June 1969): 185-202.

Brecher, Charles. *Where Have All the Dollars Gone?* New York: Praeger Publishers, 1974.

Burkhead, Jesse, with Thomas G. Fox, and John W. Holland. *Input and Output in Large-City High Schools*. Syracuse, New York: Syracuse University Press, 1967.

Burkhead, Jesse, and Jerry Miner. *Public Expenditure*. Chicago: Aldine-Atherton, 1971.

Campbell, Alan K. "Most Dynamic Sector." *National Civic Review* 52 (February 1964): 74-82.

Caro, Robert. *The Power Broker*. New York: Vintage Books, 1975.

Citizens Budget Commission, Inc. *The New York City Health and Hospitals Corporation* (October 1972).

_____. *New York City's Productivity Program: The Police Department* (November 1973).

_____. *New York City's Productivity Program: The Human Resources Administration, The Administration of Welfare* (January 1974).

_____. *New York City's Productivity Program: The Department of Sanitation* (March 1974).

Clark, Ramsey. *Crime in America*. New York: Simon and Schuster, 1970.

Committee for Economic Development. *Improving the Public Welfare System*. New York: 1970.

Cooper, Barbara S., and Nancy L. Worthington. "Age Differences in Medical Care Spending, Fiscal Year 1972." *Social Security Bulletin* 36 (May 1973): 3-15.

Costikyan, Edward N., and Maxwell Lehman. *Restructuring the Government of New York City: Report of the Scott Commission Task Force on Jurisdiction and Structure*. New York: Praeger Publishers, 1972.

Czamanski, Daniel Z. *The Cost of Preventive Services*. Lexington, Massachusetts: Lexington Books, D.C. Heath and Co., 1975.

Davis, Robert H. "Measuring Effectiveness of Municipal Services." *Management Information Service*, ICMA 2 (August 1970).

Ehrenberg, Ronald G. "The Demand for State and Local Government Employees." *American Economic Review* 63 (June 1973): 366-79.

Fitch, Lyle C., and Annmarie Hauck Walsh, eds. *Agenda for a City: Issues Confronting New York*. Beverly Hills, California: Sage Publications, 1970.

Fleisher, Belton J. "The Effect of Unemployment on Juvenile Delinquency." *Journal of Political Economy* 71 (December 1963): 543-55.

Frank, Richard S. "Economic Report/Productivity Commission Studies Techniques to Improve Public Sector Output." *National Journal* (June 10, 1972): 998-1004.

Gilpatrick, Eleanor G., and Paul K. Corless. *The Occupational Structure of New York City Municipal Hospitals*. New York: Praeger Publishers, 1970.

Greenwood, Peter W. *An Analysis of the Apprehension Activities of the New York City Police Department*. New York: New York City RAND Institute, 1970.

Hacker, Andrew. *The New Yorkers: A Profile of an American Metropolis*. New York: The Twentieth Century Fund, 1975.

Haider, Donald. "New York at the Crossroads." *City Almanac* 9 (5) (February 1975).

Hamilton, Edward K. "Productivity: The New York City Approach." *Public Administration Review* 32 (November-December 1972): 784-95.

Harris, Maryls. "Budget Bureau in a Budget Crisis." *New York Affairs* 2 (2) (1974): 20-36.

Harriss, C. Lowell. "Tax Issues in New York City." *City Almanac* 6 (5) (February 1972).

Hatry, Harry P., and Donald M. Fisk. *Improving Productivity and Productivity Measurement in Local Governments*. Washington, D.C.: The Urban Institute, June 1971.

Hirsch, Werner Z. *The Economics of State and Local Government*. New York: McGraw-Hill, 1970.

"How High Can Taxes Go?" *The New York Times*, Section IV (June 1, 1975): 1.

"How to Save New York." *Time* (October 20, 1975): 9-18.

Kegan, Lawrence R., and George P. Roniger. "The Outlook for State and Local Finance." *Fiscal Issues in the Future of Federalism*. Supplementary Paper 23. New York: Committee for Economic Development, 1968: 231-83.

Lancaster, Kelvin J. "A New Approach to Consumer Theory." *Journal of Political Economy* 74 (April 1966): 132-57.

_____. "Allocation and Distribution Theory: Technological Innovation and Progress." *American Economic Review* 56 (May 1966): 14-23.

_____. *Consumer Demand: A New Approach*. New York: Columbia University Press, 1971.

"The Last Hope." *Newsweek* (October 13, 1975): 75-78.

Levy, Frank, Arlnold J. Meltsner, and Aaron Wildavsky. *Urban Outcomes: Schools, Streets, and Libraries*. Berkeley, California: University of California Press, 1974.

Lindsay, John V. *The City*. New York: W.W. Norton and Company, 1970.

Long, Norton. "The City as Reservation." *Public Interest* 25 (Fall 1971): 22-38.

Margolis, Julius, ed. *The Analysis of Public Output*. New York: National Bureau of Economic Research, 1970.

_____. "The Demand for Urban Public Services." *Issues in Urban Economics*. Harvey S. Perloff and Lowdon Wingo, eds. Baltimore, Maryland: Johns Hopkins Press, 1968: 527-64.

Mark, Jerome A. "Meanings and Measures of Productivity." *Public Administration Review* 32 (November-December 1972): 747-53.

_____. "Progress in Measuring Productivity in Government." *Monthly Labor Review* 45 (December 1972): 3-6.

Meehan, Eugene J. "Social Indicators and Policy Analysis." *Methodologies for*

Analyzing Public Policy. Frank P. Scioli, Jr., and Thomas J. Cook, eds. Lexington, Massachusetts: Lexington Books, D.C. Heath and Co., 1975: 33-46.

Miner, Jerry. *Social and Economic Factors in Spending for Public Education.* Syracuse, New York: Syracuse University Press, 1963.

Mishan, E.J. "The Postwar Literature on Externalities: An Interpretive Essay." *Journal of Economic Literature* 9 (March 1971): 1-28.

Musgrave, R.A. *The Theory of Public Finance.* New York: McGraw-Hill, 1959.

Musgrave, R.A., and Peggy B. Musgrave. *Public Finance in Theory and Practice.* New York: McGraw-Hill, 1973.

Mushkin, Selma J., and John F. Cotton. *Functional Federalism: Grants-in-Aid and PPB Systems.* Washington, D.C.: State-Local Finances Project of The George Washington University, November 1968.

Netzer, Dick. *Economics and Urban Problems: Diagnosis and Prescriptions.* New York: Basic Books, 1970.

_____. *Economics and Urban Problems: Diagnosis and Prescriptions.* 2nd ed. New York: Basic Book, 1974.

_____. "The Cloudy Prospects for the City's Economy." *New York Affairs* 1 (Spring 1974): 22-35.

The New York Chamber of Commerce and Industry. "New York City Finances: A Ten Year Review—1963-64, 1973-74." *Real Estate News* (June-July 1974): 16-20 *et passim.*

"New York's Last Gasp?" *Newsweek* (August 4, 1975): 18-28.

Newsweek. Various issues.

New York Times. Various issues.

Nourse, Hugh O., and Donald Phares. "Socio-Economic Transition and Housing Values: A Comparative Analysis of Urban Neighborhoods." *The Social Economy of Cities*, vol. IX, Urban Affairs Annual Reviews. G. Gappert, and Harold Rose, eds. Beverly Hills, California: Sage Publications, 1975: 183-208.

Ostrom, Elinor. "Institutional Arrangements and the Measurement of Policy Consequences: Applications to Evaluating Police Performance." *Urban Affairs Quarterly* 6 (June 1971): 447-76.

_____. "On the Meaning and Measurement of Output and Efficiency in the Production of Urban Police Services." *Journal of Criminal Justice* 1 (June 1973): 93-111.

_____. "The Need for Multiple Indicators in Measuring the Output of Public Agencies." *Methodologies for Analyzing Public Policy.* Frank P. Scioli, Jr., and Thomas J. Cook, eds. Lexington, Massachusetts: Lexington Books, D.C. Heath and Co., 1975: 13-24.

Ostrom, Elinor, William H. Baugh, Richard Guarasci, Roger B. Parks, and Gordon P. Whitaker. *Community Organization and the Provision of Police Services.* Beverly Hills, California: Sage Publications, 1973.

Phares, Donald. "Assignment of Functions: An Economic Framework." *Govern-*

mental Functions and Processes. Local and Areawide. Washington, D.C.:
Advisory Commission on Intergovernmental Relations, 1974: 119-41.

———. *State-Local Tax Equity.* Lexington, Massachusetts: Lexington Books,
D.C. Heath and Co., 1973.

President's Commission on Law Enforcement and Administration of Justice. *The
Challenge of Crime in a Free Society.* Washington, D.C.: U.S. Government
Printing Office, 1967.

Ranschburg, Herbert, and Nicholas Moy. *The New York City Fire Department:
Present Achievements and Present Problems.* New York: Citizens Budget
Commission, 1973.

Report on National Needs for Criminal Justice Statistics. Washington, D.C.:
Governments Division, Bureau of the Census, August 1968.

Reischauer, Robert D., and Robert W. Hartman. *Reforming School Finance.*
Washington, D.C.: Brookings Institution, 1973.

Reiss, Albert J., Jr. "Assessing the Current Crime Wave." *Crime in Urban
Society.* Barbara N. McTenan, ed. New York: Dunellen Publishing Company,
1970.

Ridley, Clarence E., and Herbert A. Simon. *Measuring Municipal Activity.*
Chicago: International City Managers' Association, 1938.

Roniger, George. "The Economy of the New York Region." *City Almanac* 10
(1) (June 1975).

Ross, John P., and Jesse Burkhead. *Productivity in the Local Government
Sector,* Lexington, Massachusetts: Lexington Books, D.C. Heath and Co.,
1974.

Savas, E.S. "Municipal Monopoly." *Harper's Magazine* (December 1971): 55-60.

Schmandt, Henry J., and G. Ross Stephens. "Measuring Municipal Output."
National Tax Journal 13 (December 1960): 369-75.

Slavet, Joseph S., Katherine L. Bradbury, and Philip I. Moss. *Financing
State-Local Services.* Lexington, Massachusetts: Lexington Books, D.C. Heath
and Co., 1975.

Tiebout, Charles. "A Pure Theory of Local Expenditures." *Journal of Political
Economy* 64 (October 1956): 416-24.

Tyler, Humphrey S. "Stagflation: The Squeeze on Services." *Empire State
Report* (December 1974): 8-11.

Time. Various issues.

U.S. Bureau of the Census. *Census of Governments: 1972,* vol. 4, *Government
Finances.* Washington, D.C.: U.S. Government Printing Office, 1973.

U.S. Congress. Joint Economic Committee. "State-Local Finance in the Next
Decade," Dick Netzer. *Revenue Sharing and Its Alternatives: What Future for
Fiscal Federalism?* vol. II., 90th Cong., 1st sess. Washington, D.C.: U.S.
Government Printing Office, 1967: 1336-49.

U.S. Congress. Subcommittee on Intergovernmental Relations. *Criteria for
Evaluation in Planning State and Local Programs.* Washington, D.C.: U.S.
Government Printing Office, 1967.

U.S. Department of Labor. Bureau of Labor Statistics. "The Meaning of Productivity," Herbert Stein. *The Meaning and Measurement of Productivity*. Bulletin No. 1714. Washington, D.C.: U.S. Government Printing Office, 1971: 1-5.

The Urban Institute. *Measuring Solid Waste Collection Productivity*. Washington, D.C.: The Urban Institute, June 1972.

The Urban Institute and ICMA. *Measuring the Effectiveness of Basic Municipal Services*. Washington, D.C.: The Urban Institute, February 1974.

Weisman, Steven R. "How New York Became a Fiscal Junkie." *New York Times Magazine* (August 17, 1975): 8 *et passim.*

Wicksell, Knut. "A New Principle of Just Taxation." *Classics in the Theory of Public Finance*. R.A. Musgrave and A. Peacock, eds. New York: MacMillan, 1958: 72-118.

Wilson, James Q. "Do Police Prevent Crime?" *New York Times Magazine* (October 6, 1974): 18 *et passim.*

Zuccotti, John E. "Planning with Neighborhoods." *City Almanac* 9 (4) (December 1974).

Unpublished Material

Bahl, Roy, Alan Campbell, David Greytak, Bernard Jump, and Diane Lockner. "Comparative Tax Burdens in Manhattan, Queens, and Selected New York Metropolitan Area Suburbs." Occasional Paper No. 20. Syracuse University: Metropolitan Studies Program, June 1975.

City of New York. Department of Personnel. *Annual Report*. New York: Department of Personnel, Civil Service Commission, 1959 and 1969.

City of New York. Environmental Protection Administration. *Annual Progress Report and Statistical Review of the Department of Sanitation*. New York: Environmental Protection Administration, various years.

City of New York. *Expense Budget for 1971-72*. New York: City of New York, undated.

City of New York. *Schedule Supporting the Executive Budget for 1974-75*. New York: City of New York, undated.

City of New York. Department of Health. *Materia Medicaid: New York City—A Compendium of Selected Data on Trends in Medicaid 1966-71*. New York: Department of Health, August 1972.

Hospital Statistics Service. *Statistical Profile: New York City—Corporate Hospitals 1966-70 and 1969-73*. New York: Health and Hospital Corporation, undated, mimeographed.

Maxwell Research Project on the Public Finances of New York City, Working Papers #1-18, dated 1972-73.

Morley, Elaine, "The Measurement of Public Sector Activity in New York City with Reference to Police Services." Internal Working Paper #14. Syracuse University: Maxwell Research Project on the Public Finances of New York City, December 20, 1972.

Phares, Donald. "The Measurement of Public Sector Output in New York City with Reference to Sanitation." Internal Working Paper #5. Syracuse University: Maxwell Research Project on the Public Finances of New York City, August 16, 1972.

Phares, Donald, and Elaine Morley. "The Measurement of Public Sector Activity in New York City with Reference to Health and Hospitals Services." Internal Working Paper #12. Syracuse University: Maxwell Research Project on the Public Finances of New York City, November 30, 1972.

Mladenka, Kenneth R., and Kim Quaile Hill. "The Distribution of Urban Police Services." Prepared for delivery at the annual meeting of the Midwest Political Science Association, Pick-Congress Hotel, Chicago, Illinois, May 1-3, 1975.

Parks, Robert B. "Measurement of Performance in the Public Sector: A Case Study of the Indianapolis Police Department," Bloomington, Indiana: Indiana University, Department of Political Science, Workshop in Political Theory and Policy Analysis, 1971.

Reiss, Albert J., Jr. "Studies in Crime and Law Enforcement in Major Metropolitan Areas." University of Michigan, undated.

Index

Index

activities, as facets of output, 14, 16n
Adaptive Response System, 55
AFDC, 61-62, 65, 66, 111
affiliation agreements, 70
Allison, John, 107n
allocation, 5
arson, 55
assignment, fiscal, 6, 9, 120
attributes of goods, 16

Bahl, Roy, 30n, 89, 106n
Baumol, William, 17n, 113n, 122n
Baumol's disease, relation to output
  measurement, 12, 114
Bish, Robert, 3n, 17n
Blum, Edward H., 55n, 107n
bond anticipation notes, 117, 119
borough population characteristics,
  91-97
Brackett, Jean, 96n
Bradford, D.F., 14, 17n
Brecher, Charles, 30n, 68n, 70n
Bronx, 89, 91-97, 129-163
Brooklyn, 89, 91-97, 129-163
Bureau of Labor Statistics, 96n
Burkhead, Jesse, 10n, 14n

Campbell, Alan K., 6, 17n, 30n
Carey, Governor, 117
Caro, Robert, 114n
central cities, as reservations, 29
characteristics, Lancaster's view of
  goods, 15
citizen, awareness of government's
  impact, 11
Citizens Budget Commission, 46n,
  77n, 122n
City University of New York, 114,
  120
Clark, Ramsey, 35n
clearance rates, 45-47
common functions, definition, 24, 25t
commuters, impact on public services,
  21, 97
Cooper, Barbara, 107n
C-output, 14
Corless, Paul, 77n
crime: clearance rates, 45-47; and

population characteristics, 89; underreporting, 35; victimless, 36. *See
also* Police Department

Davis, Robert, 11, 64
debt: cost of servicing, 23; per capita
  burden of, 119; short term, 119
decentralization, 115-116
default, 117, 118, 121
deficits on budget, 117, 118, 119-120
Department of Sanitation (DOS):
  budget, 21-23; cost compared to
  private collection, 112; data by borough, 157-163; data sources, 79n,
  128; employment, 21-23, 79; functions, 79; incorporation into Environmental Protection Administration, 79; maintenance of vehicles,
  85-86; output measurement, 80;
  peak load scheduling, 85; performance measurement, 83-85; refuse
  collected, 79; refuse disposal, 83;
  snow and ice removal, 82; street
  cleaning, 79-81; supportive activities,
  83; towing operations, 82-83, 85
Department of Social Services (DSS).
  See social services
Depression, the, 28
determinants of public expenditures,
  studies of, 9-10, 12-14
distribution, 5
dollars, as a measure of public activity,
  6, 10, 12-14
Dopkeen, Jonathan, 86n
D-output, 14
Dreisbach-Williams, Roger, 86n
drug addiction, 61-62, 69, 71, 73, 76

economies of scale, relation to output,
  xvii, 5, 7n
education, 23, 25-27
effectiveness, definition, 11
efficiency, definition, 11
Ehrenberg, Ronald, 107n
Elmore, Thomas, 116n
Environmental Protection Administration, 79, 83
equality, relation to output, xvii, 5

177

About the Authors

David Greytak is associate professor of economics in the Maxwell School of Citizenship and Public Affairs at Syracuse University. He was a codirector of the Maxwell Project on the Public Finances of New York City and currently serves as the director of the Urban Transportation Institute and associate director of the Metropolitan Studies Program at Syracuse University. Dr. Greytak has written in the areas of urban and regional economics and public finance, and has published in the *Journal of Regional Science, National Tax Journal, Traffic Quarterly, Public Administration Review, Regional and Urban Economics, Annals of Regional Science*, and *Regional Studies*. He is also a coauthor of the book *Taxes, Expenditures, and the Economic Base* (with Roy Bahl and Alan Campbell). Dr. Greytak holds the B.A. from St. Edward's University in Austin, Texas, and an M.A. and a Ph.D. from Washington University in St. Louis. He was also a postdoctoral fellow in the Institute for Applied Urban Economics at Indiana University.

Donald Phares is associate professor of economics and a fellow in the Center of Community and Metropolitan Studies at the University of Missouri-St. Louis. He is author of the book *State-Local Tax Equity: An Empirical Analysis of the Fifty States*, articles in *Social Science Quarterly, Proceedings of the National Tax Association, Annals of Regional Science, Journal of Regional Science, Economic Geography, Journal of Drug Issues, Journal of Psychedelic Drugs*, sections in several books, and government reports. His research deals primarily with drug abuse, housing and neighborhood change, and state-local finance and governmental structure. He holds the B.A. from Northeastern University in Boston, Massachusetts and an M.A. and a Ph.D. from Syracuse University, Syracuse, New York.

Elaine Morley is a Ph.D. candidate in the Social Science Program, the Maxwell School, Syracuse University. She was a member of the research staff for the Maxwell Research Project on the Public Finances of New York City and has been a research assistant at the Metropolitan Studies Program, Syracuse University.